# HOW TO DRAW
# KAWAII

Learn to Draw Super Cute Stuff -
Animals, Chibi, Magical Creatures,
Food, Flowers, Items and More!

How to Draw Kawaii
© 2020
All Rights Reserved

No part of this book may be reproduced, stored in a retrieval system, or transmitted by any means without the written permission of the author and publisher.

Thank you for getting our book!

If you enjoy using it and you found it useful in your journey of learning to draw, we would greatly appreciate your review on Amazon.

Just head on over to this book's Amazon page and click "Write a customer review".

We read each and every one of them. Thanks!

# CONTENTS

Introduction .................................................................................................................. 1
**Kawaii People** ........................................................................................................... 2
    Chibi ...................................................................................................................... 2
    Chibi Drawing Tips .............................................................................................. 6
        Eye Shape Variation ..................................................................................... 7
        Facial Expressions ....................................................................................... 9
    Chibi Counterparts ............................................................................................ 10
**Kawaii Animals** ...................................................................................................... 14
    Birds ................................................................................................................... 28
    Sea Creatures .................................................................................................... 35
    Fish ..................................................................................................................... 35
    Octopus .............................................................................................................. 36
    Turtle .................................................................................................................. 37
    Shark .................................................................................................................. 38
    Whale ................................................................................................................. 39
    Dolphin .............................................................................................................. 40
    Tall Animals ...................................................................................................... 41
    Llama ................................................................................................................. 41
    Giraffe ................................................................................................................ 43
    Ostrich ............................................................................................................... 45
**Kawaii Plants** ......................................................................................................... 47
    Leaves ................................................................................................................ 47
    Flowers .............................................................................................................. 51
    Rosebud ............................................................................................................. 51
    Rose .................................................................................................................... 52
    Daisy ................................................................................................................... 53
    Tulip .................................................................................................................... 54
    Sunflower .......................................................................................................... 55
    Cherry Blossom ................................................................................................ 56
    House Plants ..................................................................................................... 57

**Kawaii Creatures** ............................................................................................................ 61
    Unicorn ..................................................................................................................... 61
    Mermaids ................................................................................................................. 63
    Pegasus .................................................................................................................... 65
    Fairies ....................................................................................................................... 67
    Dragon ..................................................................................................................... 69

**Kawaii Objects** ................................................................................................................. 71
    Boy's Things ............................................................................................................ 71
    Girl's Things ............................................................................................................ 79
    School Things ......................................................................................................... 85
    Furniture ................................................................................................................. 91
    Kitchen Things ....................................................................................................... 97
    Bathroom Things ................................................................................................. 103
    Cleaning Things ................................................................................................... 109
    Beach Things ........................................................................................................ 115
    Fitness And Sports .............................................................................................. 121
    Travel Things ....................................................................................................... 127

**Final Words** ................................................................................................................... 128

# INTRODUCTION

Kawaii is a japanese word which means cute, lovable, and adorable. But, it is more than just a direct translation of the word cute.

Kawaii is actually a very wide and popular culture.

Kawaii can be found in almost anything and everything! It can be your clothes, toys, food, animals, and even everyday objects you can find inside your home!

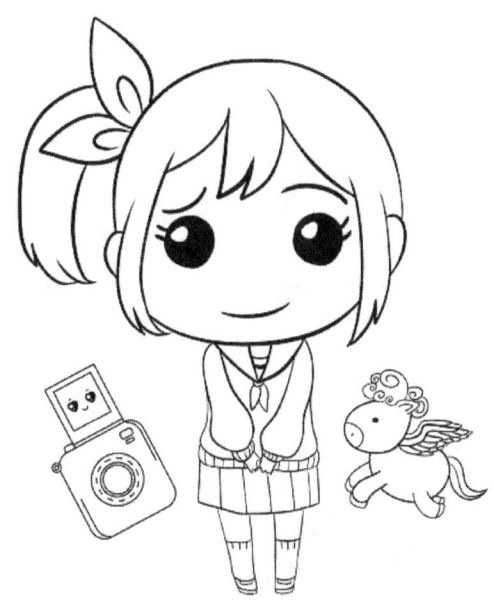

The first use of the word actually dates back to the period wherein the word kawaii means pitiable, and is usually used to describe women.

The rise of cuteness in Japan as a culture began during the 1970s when cute handwriting rose in popularity amongst teenage girls.

Written characters were drawn big and rounded and small pictures like hearts, stars, cartoon characters and faces were added.

Later on, this style of writing was adopted into magazines, packaging designs, comics, and then into merchandise. The kawaii aesthetic became so popular that it has become a subculture in and of itself and can be found all-over Japan.

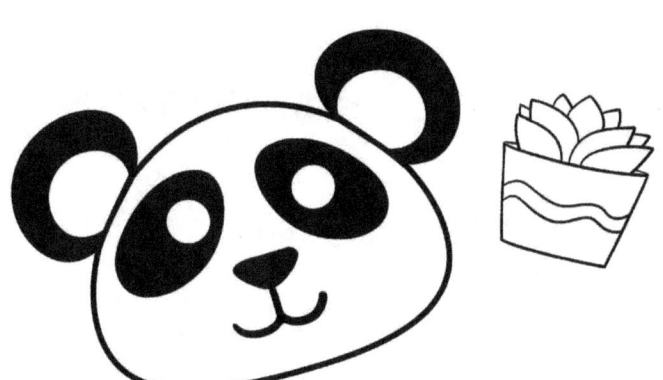

In these tutorials, we will be going over on how to draw everything kawaii!

So get your pencils and let's start drawing!

# KAWAII PEOPLE
## CHIBI

Chibi in Japanese is a slang that is used to describe something or someone that is short.

In drawing, chibi is a caricature style of drawing characters known for its oversized head and small and short body and limbs.

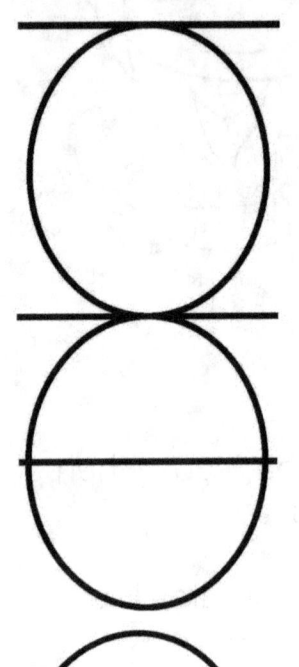

The usual body proportion for a chibi character is usually measured by 2 heads' size wherein the size of the head depends on you.

The first head size is the head of the character while the second head size is the whole body including the arms and legs of the character.

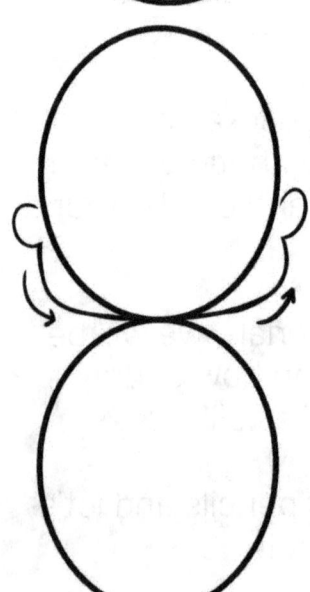

Start off by drawing a curved line that starts from halfway of the first head size down, this will be the lower half of the face of our chibi.

Smaller curves on each side of the face are the ears, make them bigger or smaller to create unique facial features.

Remember that drawing chibi characters require rounded body parts!

Avoid sharp and straight lines when adding features.

Add the chibi's eyes by drawing a pair of rounded rectangles with a pair of eyebrows on top of it.

You can make the eyes as simple as you can, even a pair of simple circles would do!

Eyebrows play a big part in showing the character's emotions.

Make sure to play with the eyebrow's shapes to portray various feelings.

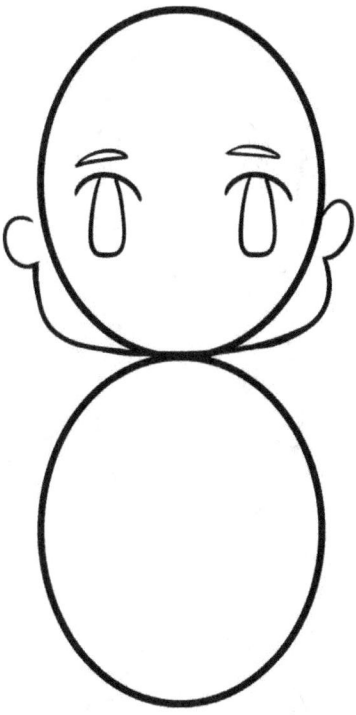

Add the mouth of the chibi. Like the eyebrows, the mouth will convey the emotions of the character we are drawing!

Draw simple lines as mouth shapes for various emotions.

Draw the hair of the chibi starting from the top most part of the first head size down to the ears.

The key in drawing hair for chibi characters is to draw it as simplified as you can!

Details such as hair strands are not required when drawing chibi characters.

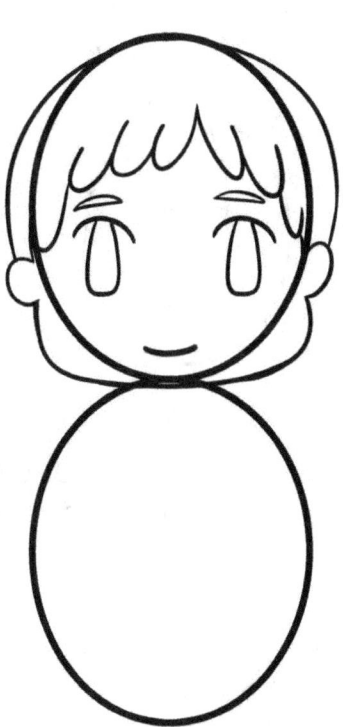

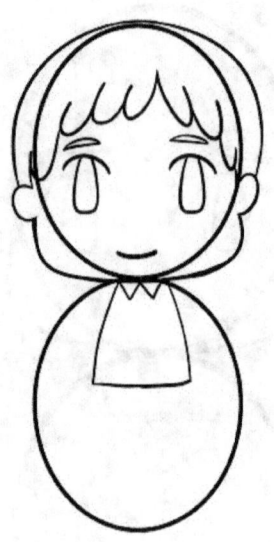

Draw the torso of the chibi by adding a simple shape starting from the top side of the second head shape down.

According to your preferences, you can make the chibi's torso longer or shorter. Making a shorter torso will make longer legs and vice versa.

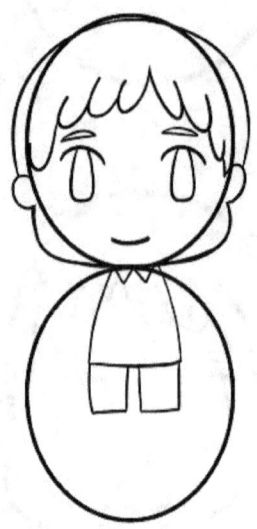

In the example, the chibi character will be wearing a pair of shorts.

Add the bottom garment from the edge of the torso downwards.

Add a pair of arms at each side of the torso. Draw the hands at the end of each arm.

Remember that body parts and facial features are not very detailed when drawing chibi characters!

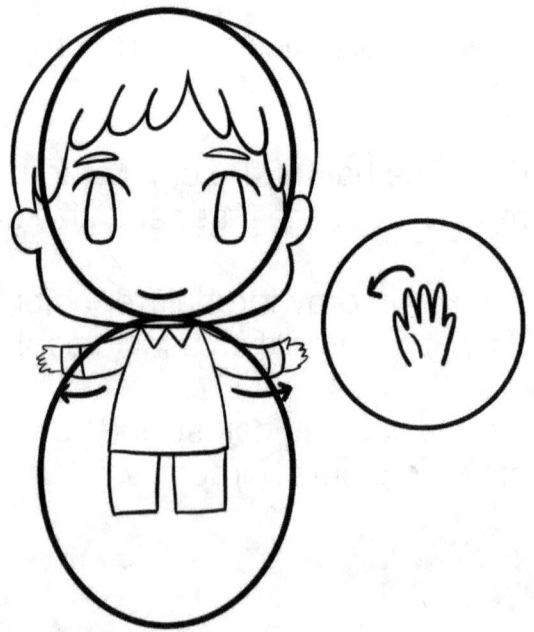

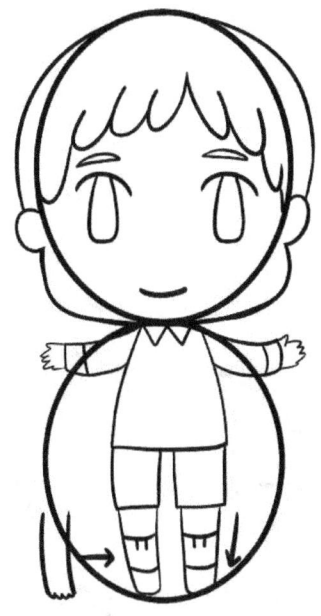

Add the legs at the end of the character's bottom clothing.

If you want your character to be wearing long bottom clothes like pants or leggings, then draw them like the legs in the example.

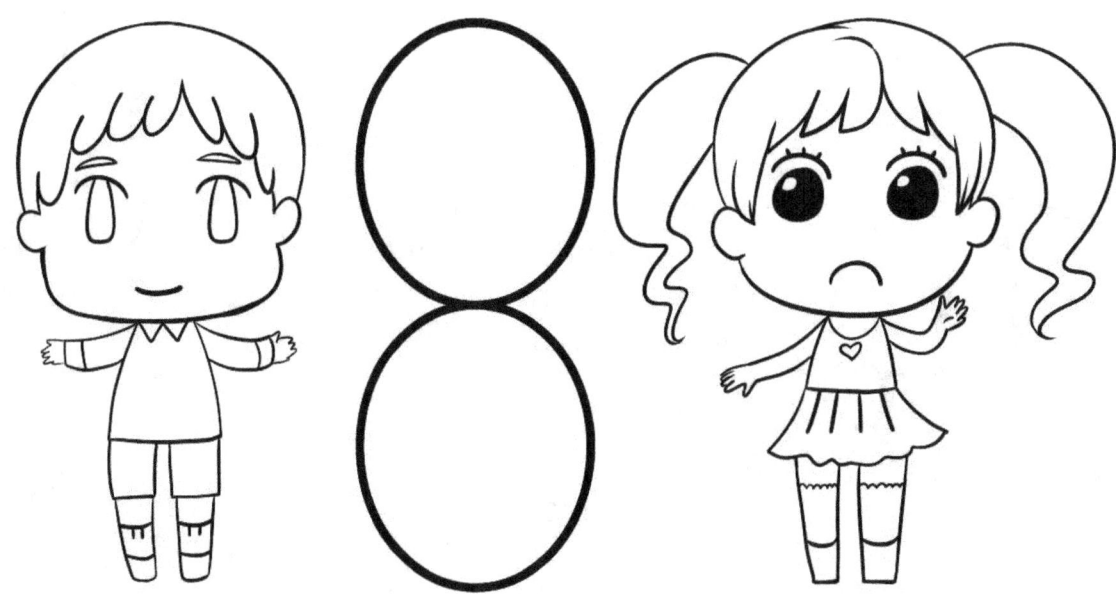

And you are done drawing your chibi character!

Create variations with their hairstyles, facial features and expressions, as well as their clothing.

The most important thing to remember is to follow the two head size proportion in drawing chibi.

# KAWAII PEOPLE
# CHIBI DRAWING TIPS

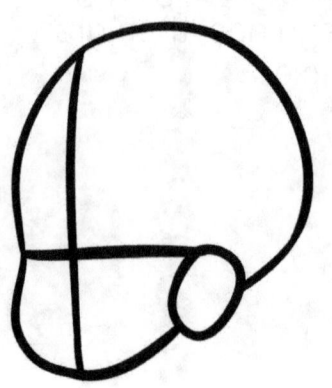

Drawing the side view of a chibi would only show one side of the head and the body.

The same two-head size proportion is still applied to the side view.

An important tip to remember is to draw the below the eye and to make sure that the arm and the leg are parallel to each other.

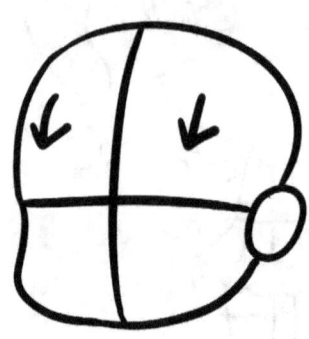

In the three-quarters view of the character, it looks a bit like the front view but a small portion of the body is not visible.

The same proportion is applied to this view.

Make sure that the eyes of the character follow the placing as pointed by the arrowheads in the example, drawing them too close to each other or too far apart will make the chibi look weird.

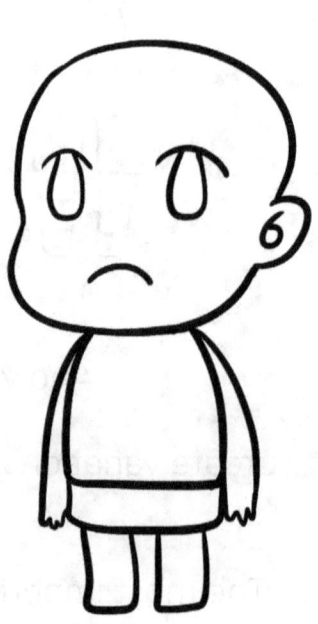

# EYE SHAPE VARIATION

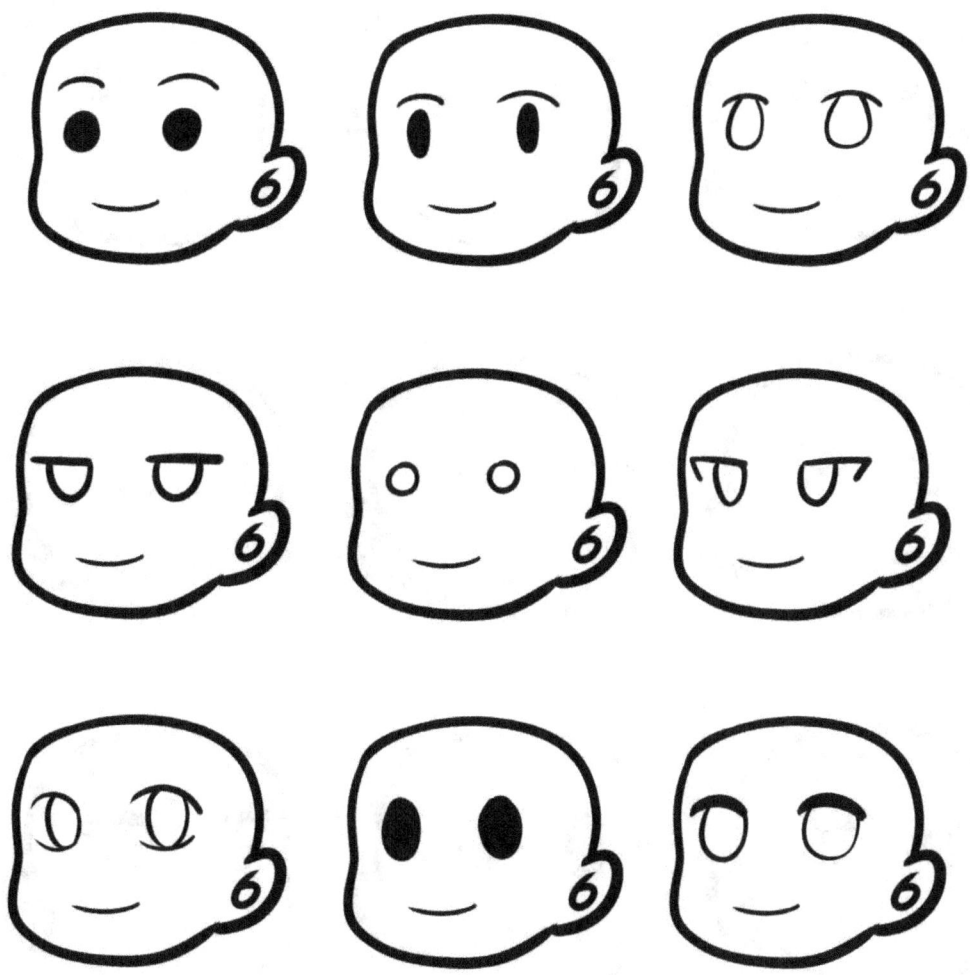

Here are some eye shape variations that can help you draw more interesting and unique chibi characters!

Remember that the eyes are important in showing your character's personality!

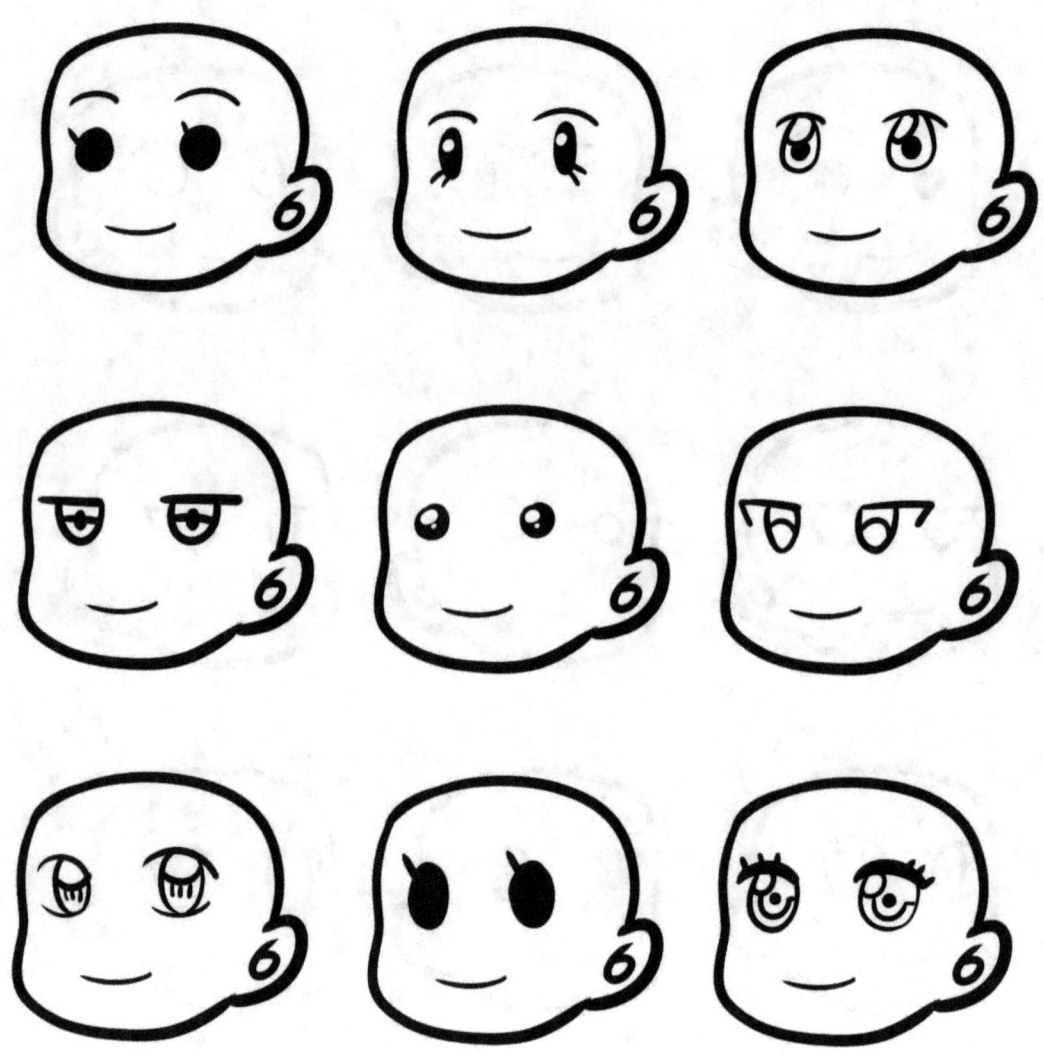

Adding small details in the eyes like lashes, shapes, and sparkles can even make your character more alive and unique!

Be creative and think about how will simple shapes can bring your chibi to life.

# FACIAL EXPRESSIONS

Since chibi characters have the same facial features as normal characters (except the nose!), you can show a variety of expressions that will enhance your chibi's emotions!

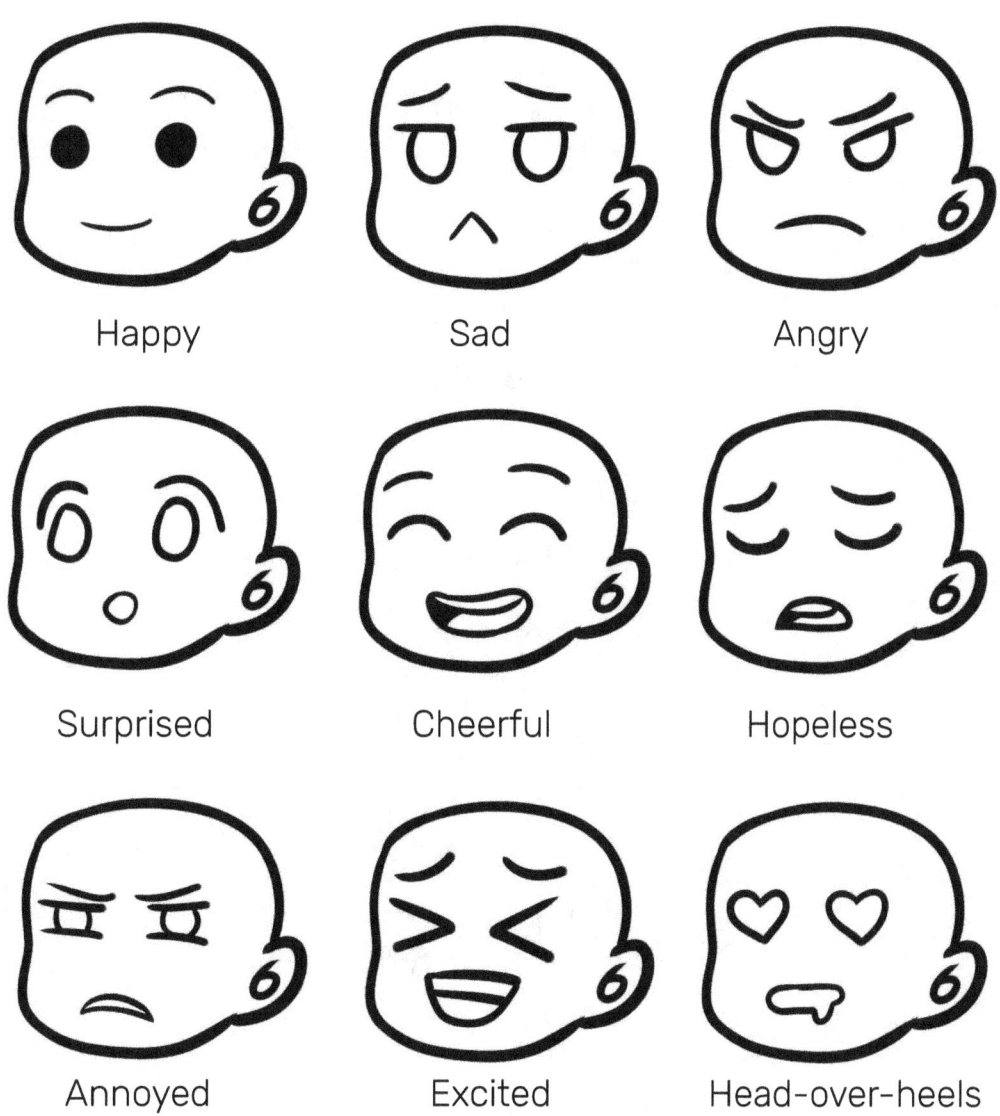

Happy　　　　Sad　　　　Angry

Surprised　　　　Cheerful　　　　Hopeless

Annoyed　　　　Excited　　　　Head-over-heels

# KAWAII PEOPLE
## CHIBI COUNTERPARTS

Since we already covered the basics in drawing chibi characters, it is now time to see how existing characters look like in chibi style!

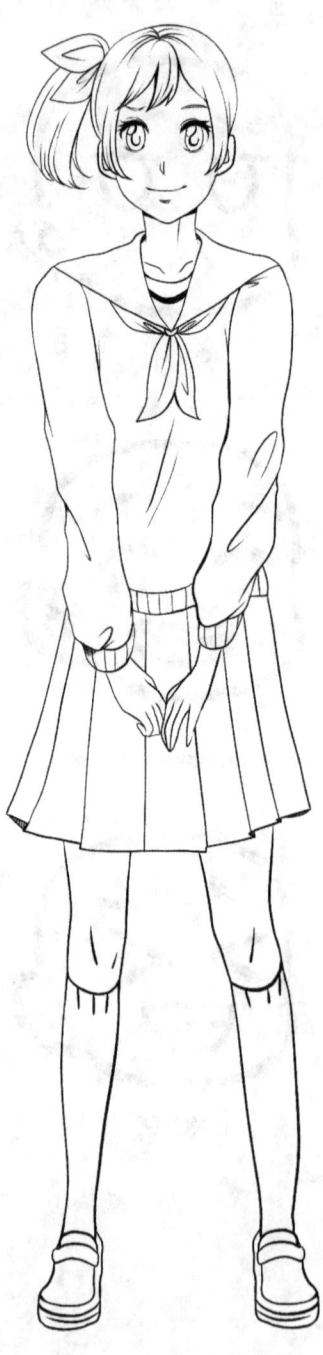

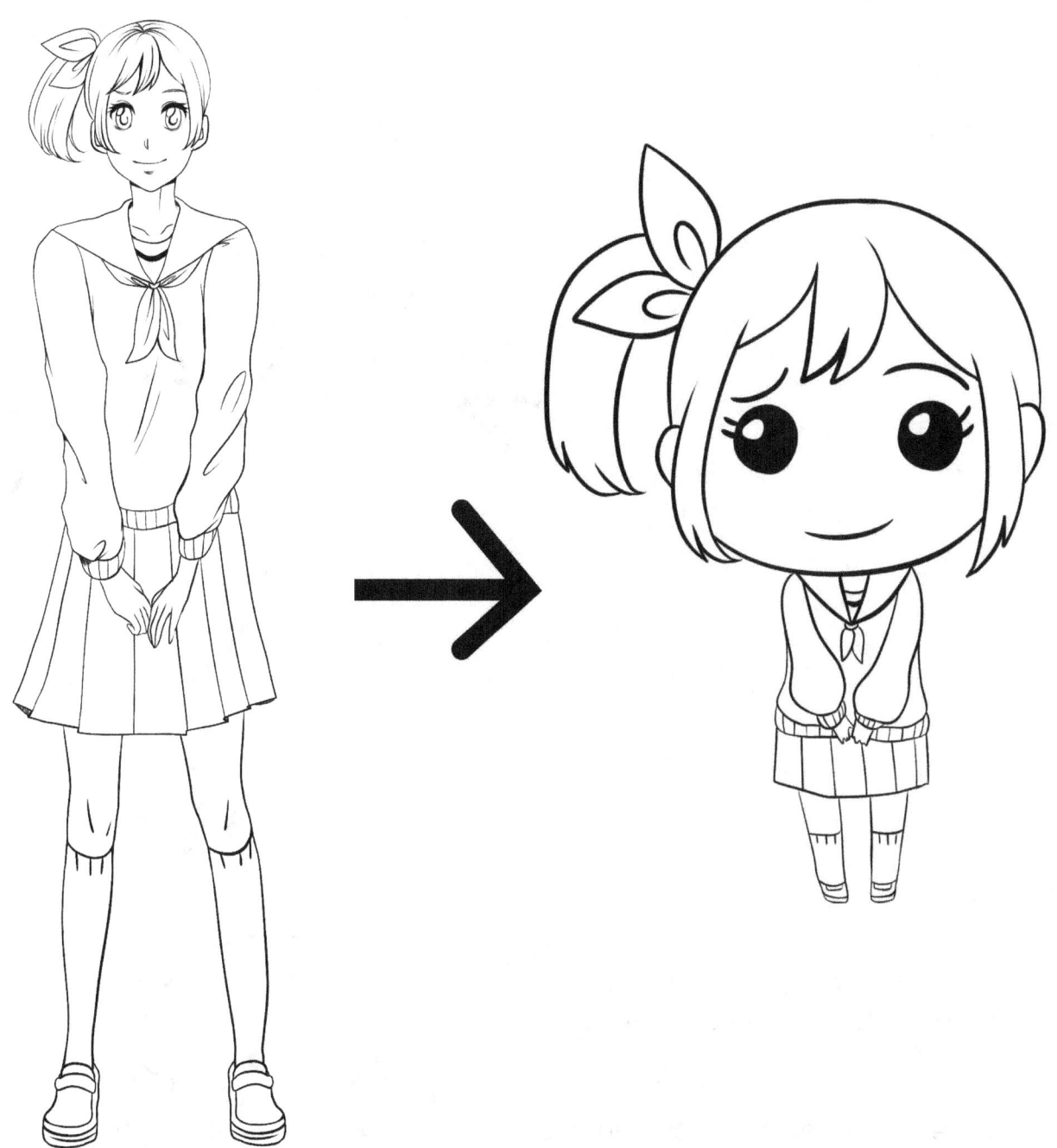

Take note of how the details were translated into the chibi character's design:

The hair strand details were not included.
The clothes' folds were also not included.
The sweater was still drawn to look loose on the character
by adding more curves.
The shoes' design was simplified.

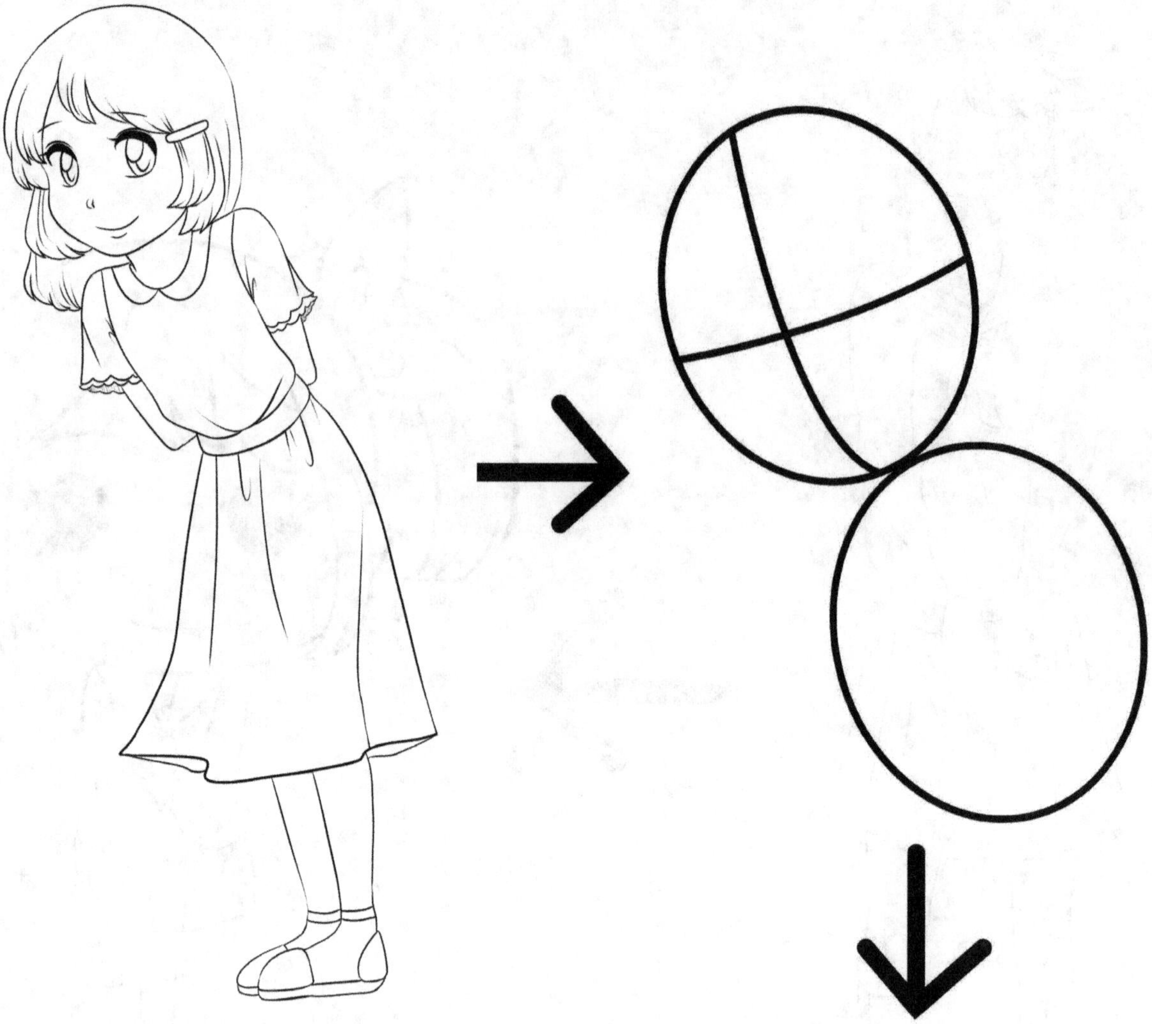

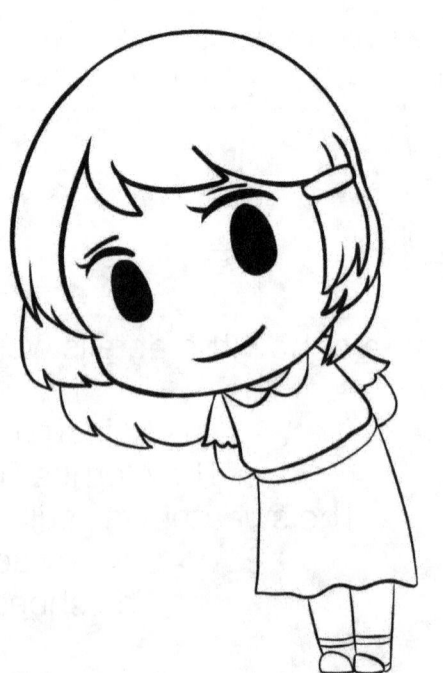

Like the first character that we did; simplify the details of the chibi like the hair and the folds.

Even if the character is standing in a pose, make sure to follow the two-heads proportion for chibis!

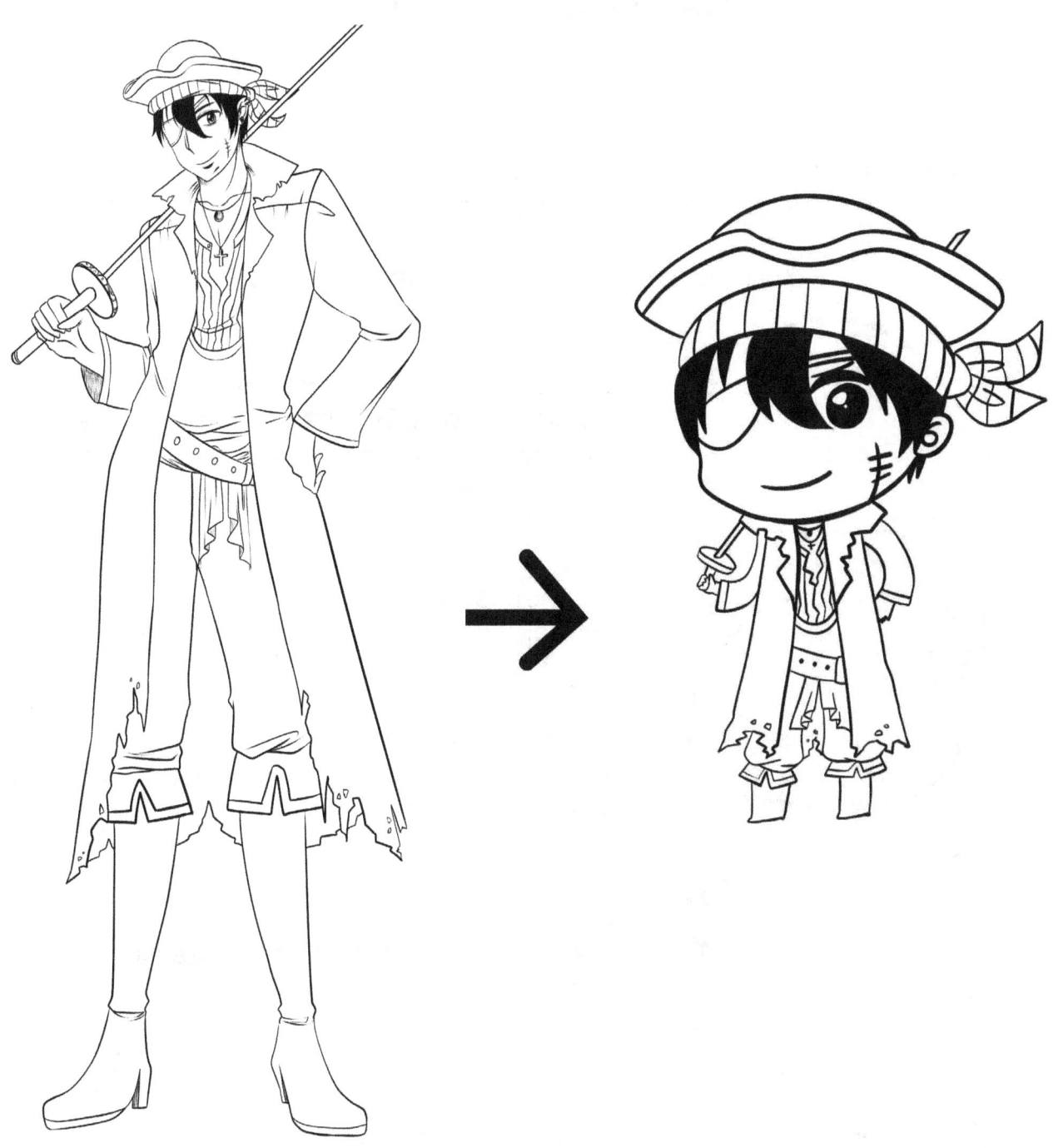

For designs with a bit more complicated details; think about which details are important and are needed to keep the character itself.

Like in this example, the striped bandanna, the necklaces, the torn coat, the high boots and the rapier were kept so that the character remains looking like a pirate.

# KAWAII ANIMALS

Drawing kawaii animals is easy!

Like drawing chibis the main key point in making animals look cute is to make sure that the features are rounded and the details are simplified.

We will start in drawing simple animal heads!

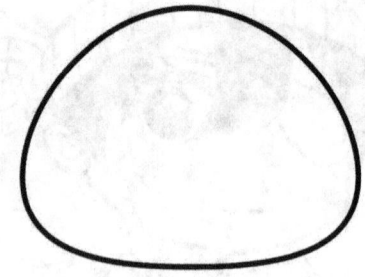

The first step is to draw a shape with rounded edges. This basic shape can be used for various animals from cats to dogs and even birds!

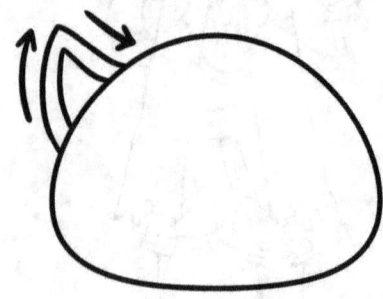

The next step is to draw the ear of the animal.

This example is a cat so the ears are pointed like triangles. Various animals have different ear shapes. Add a slight curve when drawing the ears so that it would not look unnatural.

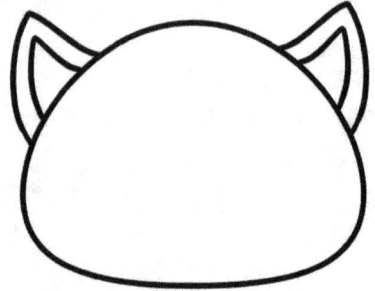

Draw another ear at the opposite side of the first ear.

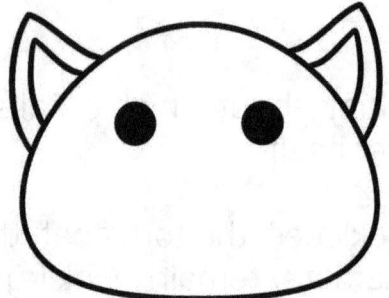

Add a pair of eyes by drawing two circles slightly below the ears of the cat. You can modify the shape of the eyes like those of the chibis.

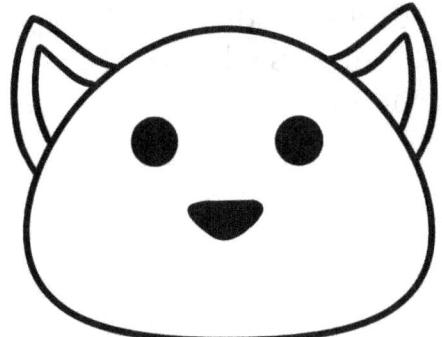

Draw a nose which is shaped like an inverted triangle with rounded edges.

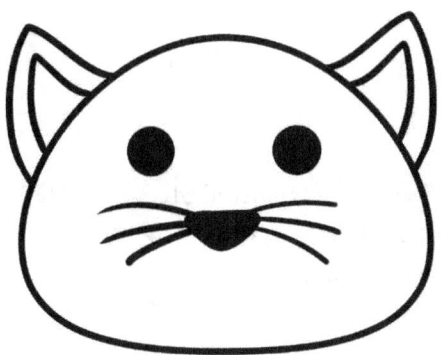

Add facial features to the cat like the whiskers. You can also add some patterns on the fur or even accessories on the top of its head!

The same process will be done to draw other animals.
The only difference would be the specific facial features which will differentiate one animal from the other.

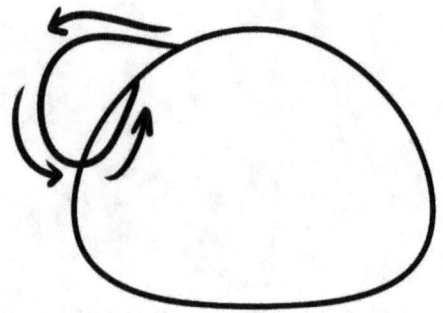

When drawing stylized dogs, their ears are usually droopy and very rounded.

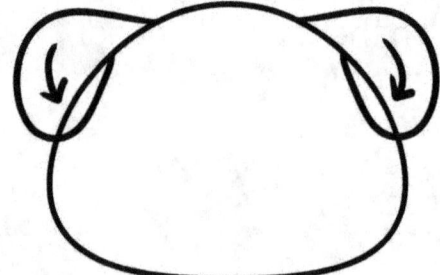

Draw another one at the opposite side of the head and erase the lines where the ears and head intersect.

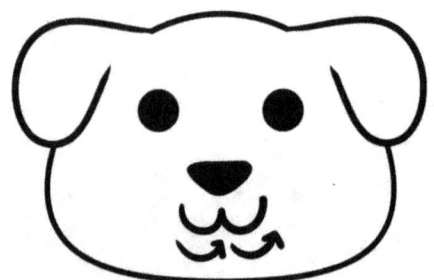

Draw the eyes and the nose.
You can draw a cute mouth too.

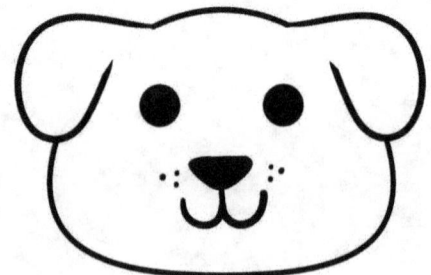

And the dog is now done!

Adding more details will make it look a lot cuter!

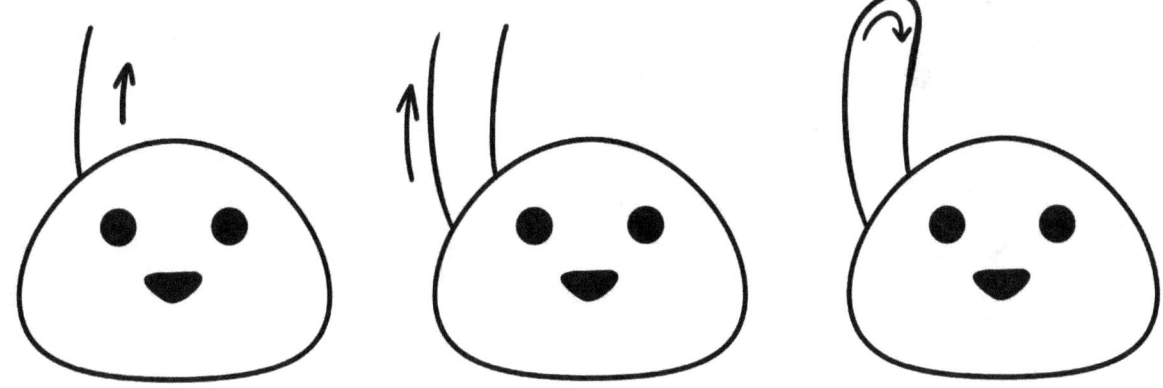

Draw bunny ears upwards and as high as you want them to be, remember the rounded edge!

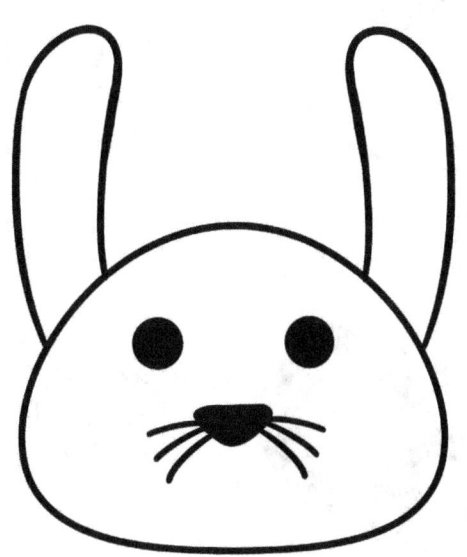

Don't forget to add the final details.

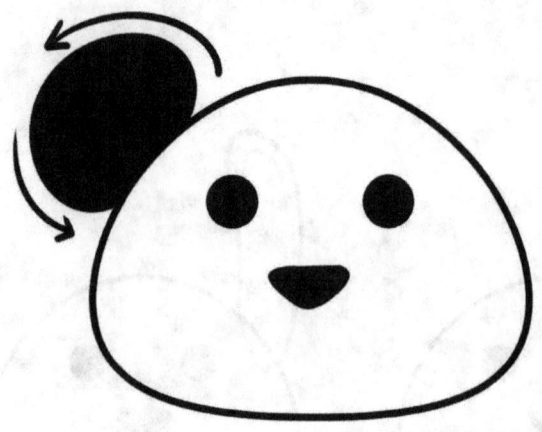

Panda ears on the other hand are big, rounded and black.

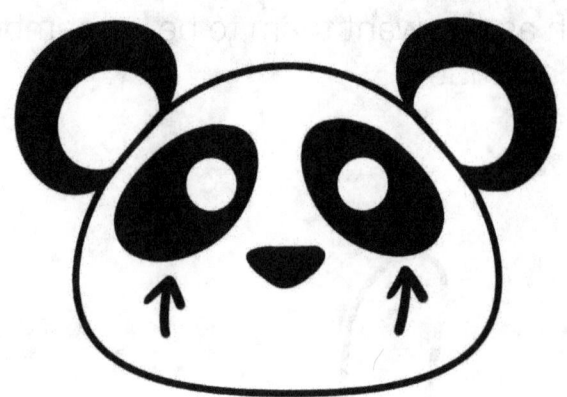

Draw the other ear of the panda and add white circles inside of the black ones.

The eyes of the panda are white and black patches are around them.

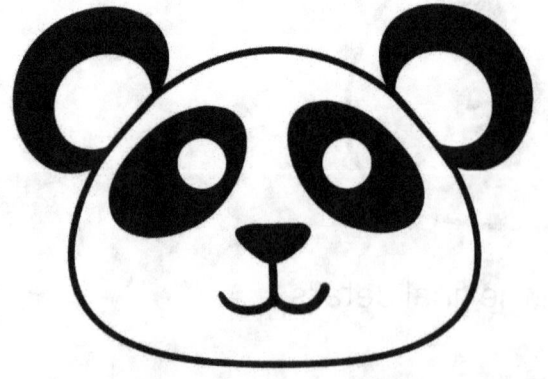

As always, add the last details of the panda! And you're done with your kawaii panda!

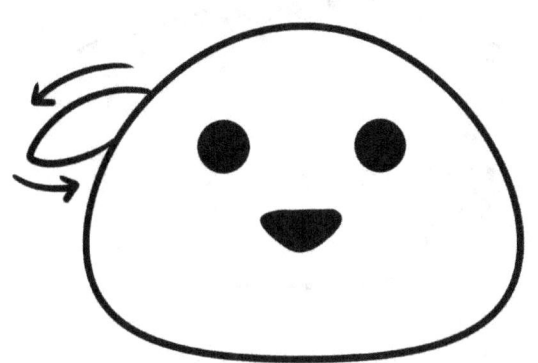

Some animals have small and slightly pointed ears.

In this example, we will be drawing a sheep!

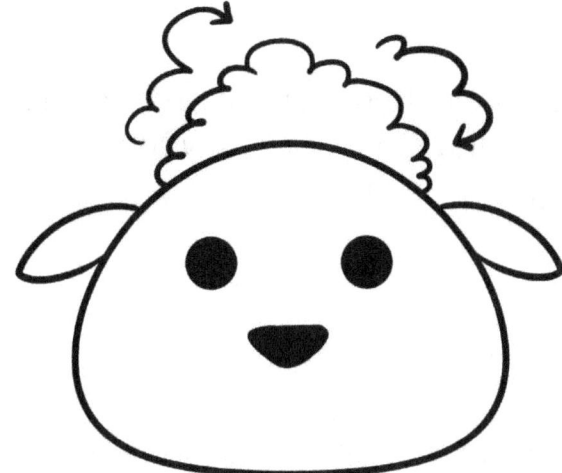

Draw a fluffy patch of wool on top of its head using curved lines like clouds.

And your kawaii sheep is now done!

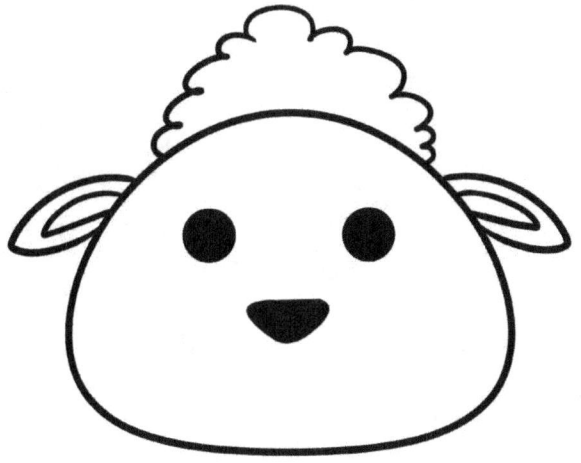

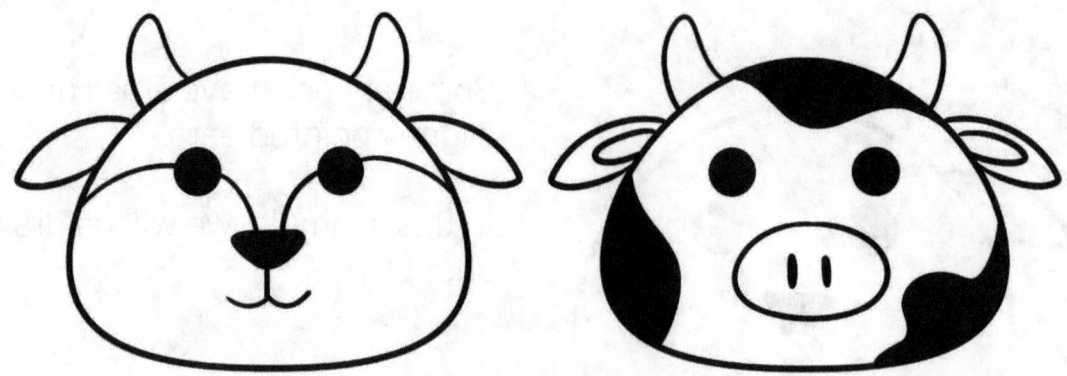

Other animals that have the same ears as the sheep are deer and cow!

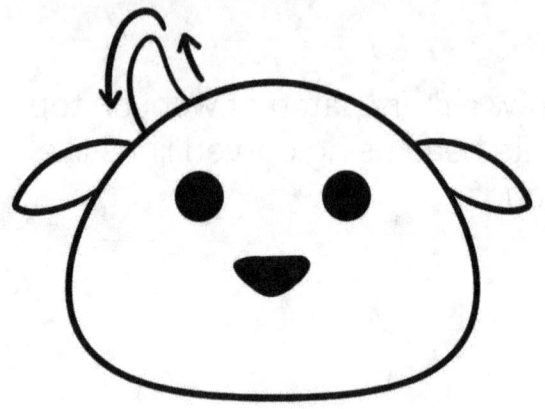

Both have horns which are drawn in short and upward lines with a rounded edge.

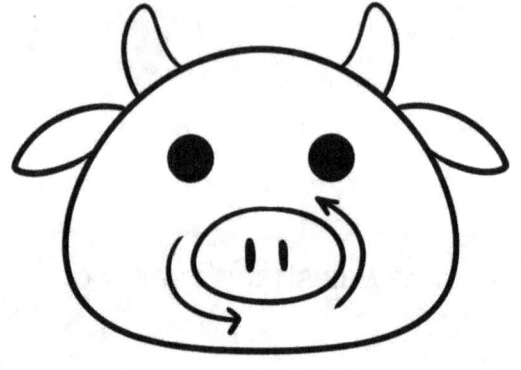

Cows on the other hand have big snouts rather than small noses.

We draw them with an oval with a pair of lines in the middle.

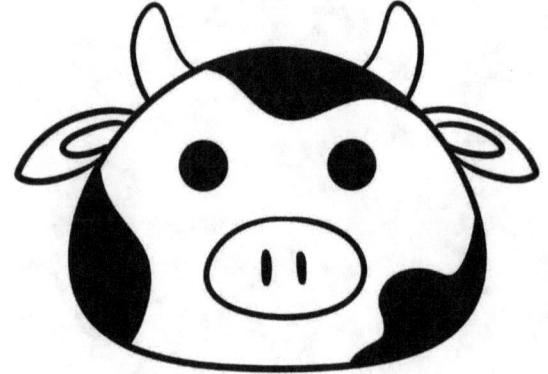

Cows also have black splotches as patterns.

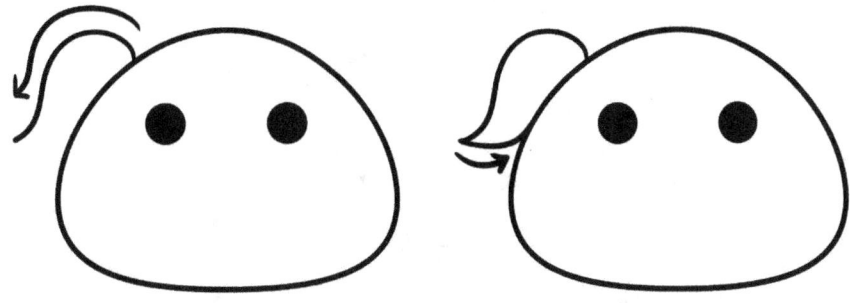

Pigs have curled up ears that are shaped like leaves.

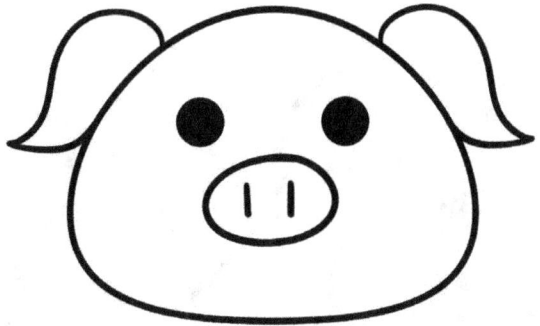

They also have snouts instead of noses!

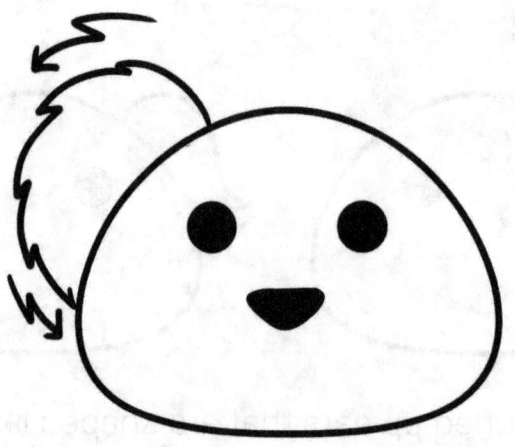

Koalas have furry and wide ears!

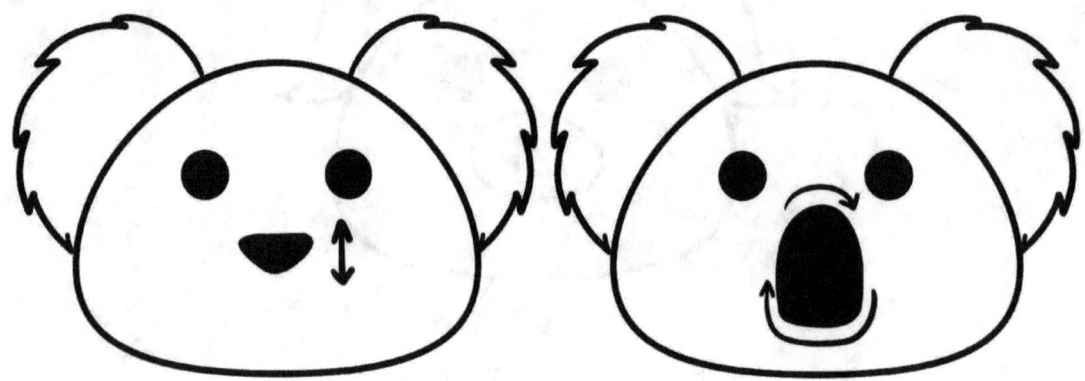

They have long and wide noses instead of cute little ones.

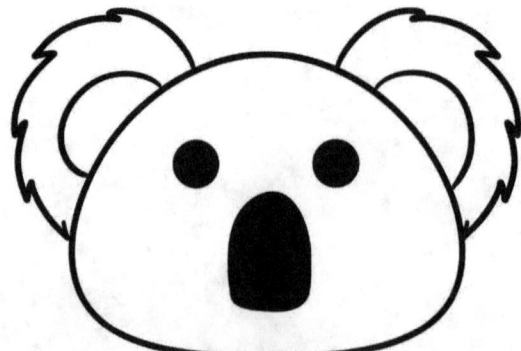

Don't forget to add the other finishing touches such as the inner ears!

# KAWAII ANIMALS

Now that we have covered the steps in drawing the heads of cute animals, the next step would be to draw the whole body!

Like chibis, animals are drawn with as little details as possible and very rounded body parts.

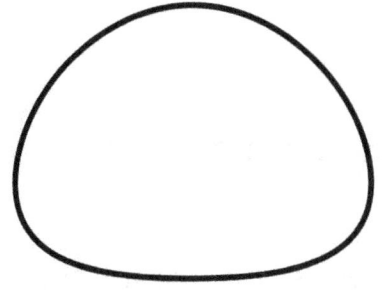

We will start with the same shape that we used in drawing the heads of animals.

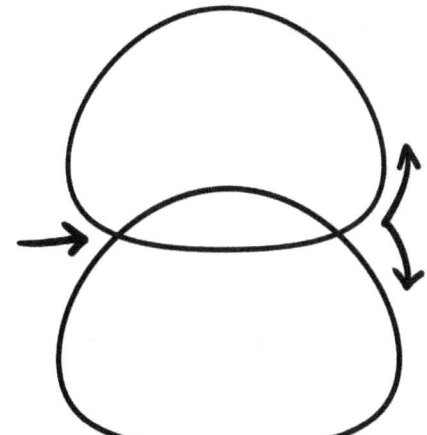

Place another rounded shape at the top of the first one. The one at the top would be the head and the one at the bottom would be the body.

Make sure that the head is a bit smaller than the body and that both shapes intersect with each other.

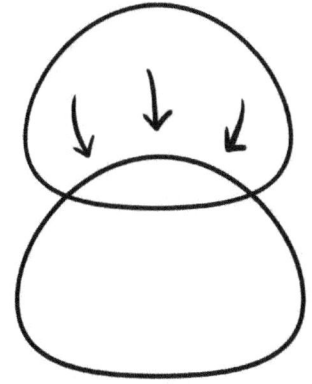
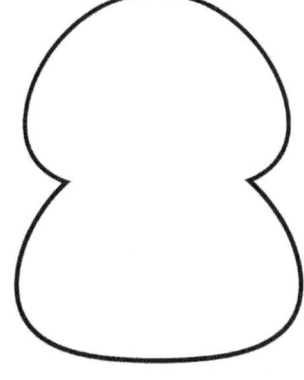

Erase the intersecting lines so that the two shapes will look like a single shape!

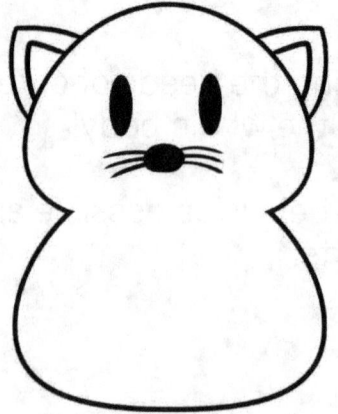

Draw the facial features in the head of the animal following the same process as in the head tutorial.

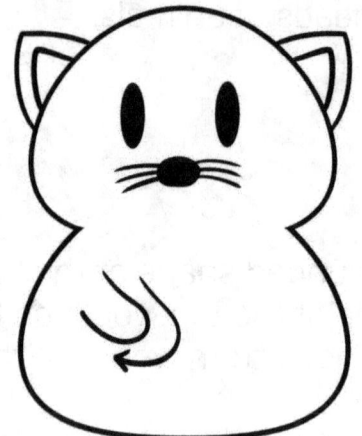

Next we add the little arms of this kawaii cat.

A simple and rounded arm just below the neck.

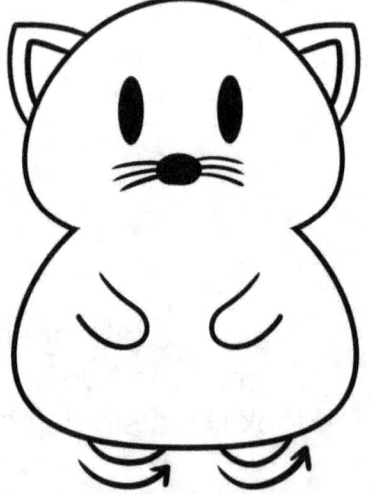

Draw the other arm opposite of the first one.

Add a pair of little feet by drawing two curves below the body.

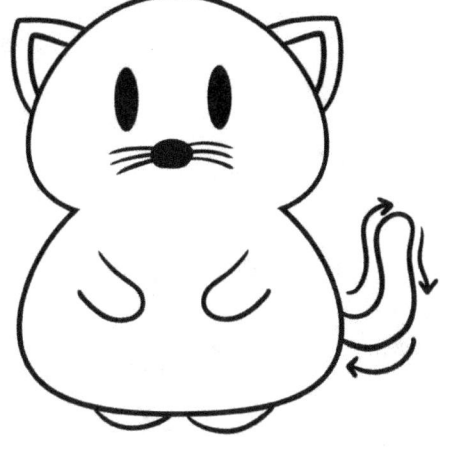

Add the tail at one side of the body.

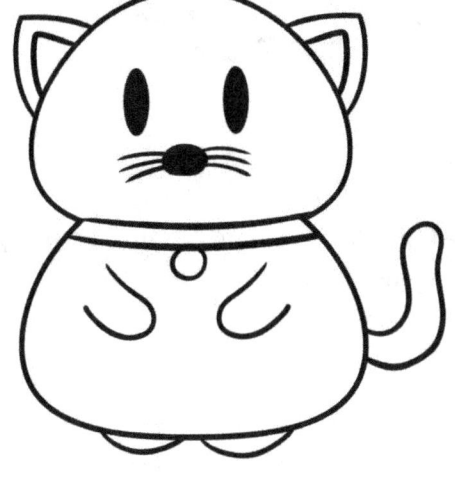

And your kawaii cat is now done!
You can even add some accessories like a cute collar!

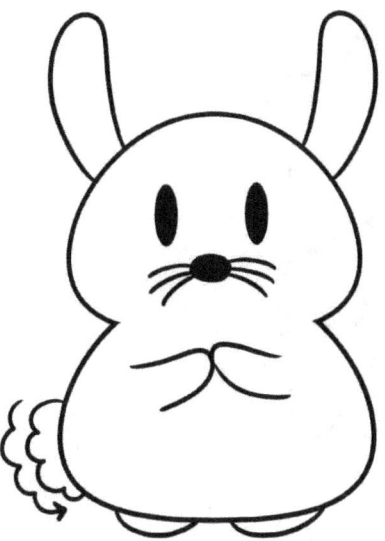

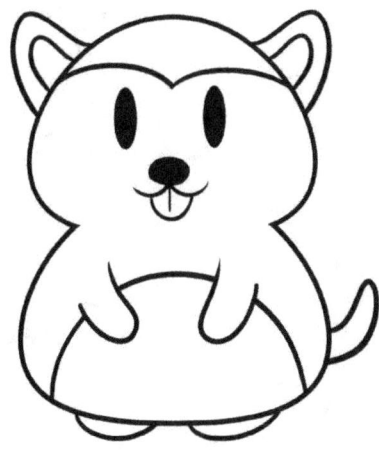

Here are more examples of animals drawn with the same body shape!
Add body patterns and don't forget to draw their ears and other body parts such as the tail accordingly!
Bunnies have fluffy and short tails while some dogs have pointed tails!

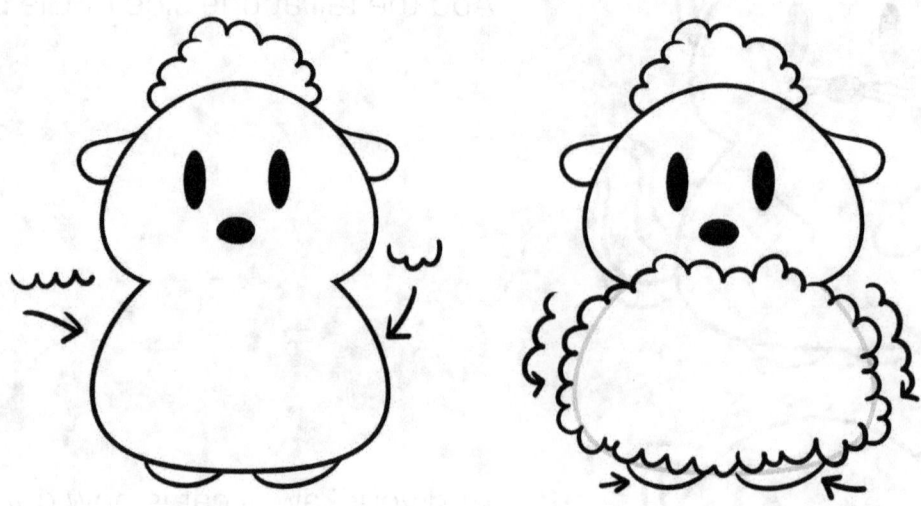

Some animals' bodies are covered with fur!
For example, a sheep is mostly covered in fluffy wool.
Draw the wool around the body making sure to add variation with the sizes of the curves to make it look cute!

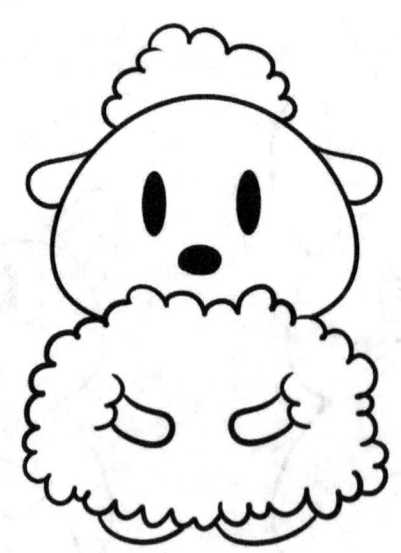

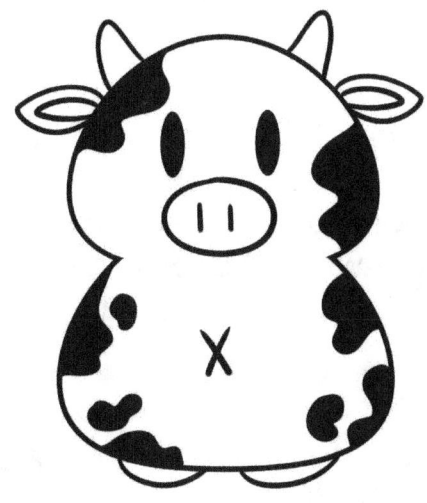

Some animals' bodies have patterns all over!
Most of the patterns are not visible in the middle part!

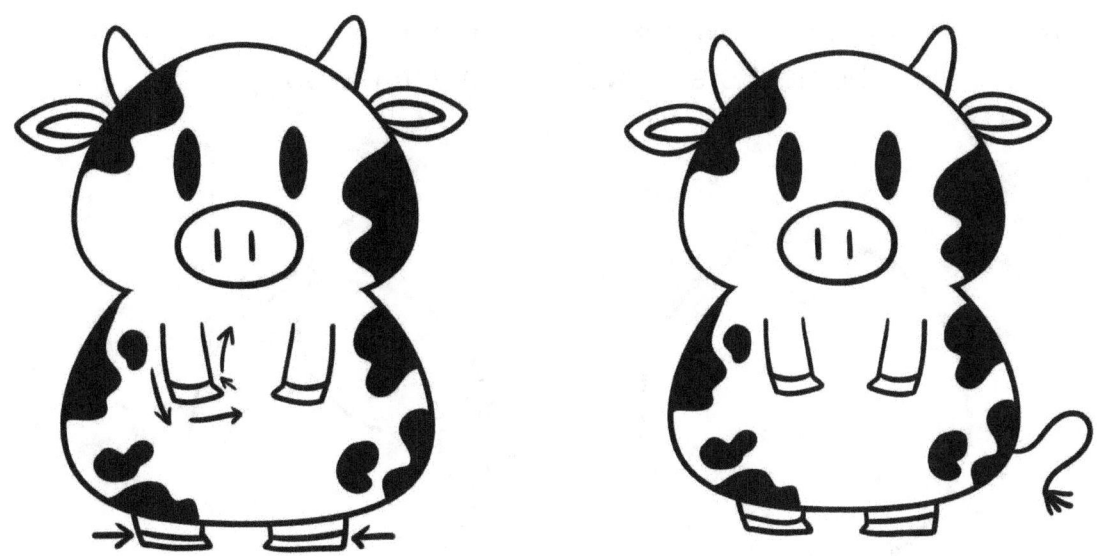

Animals like cows also have hooves, so instead of rounded arms
we will draw a flat one.

# KAWAII ANIMALS
## BIRDS

For this tutorial, we will focus on our feathered friends!
We can draw birds using the same method as in our previous tutorials
but we will look at other body shapes
that will suit birds better!

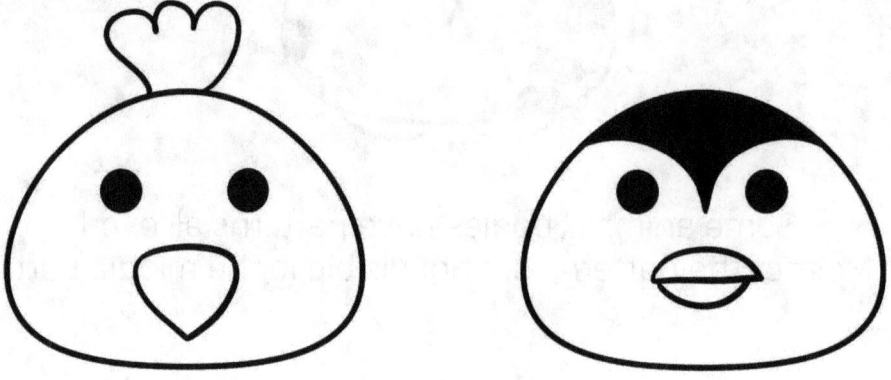

Here are examples of a chicken and a penguin using the first tutorial we did!
For the next steps, we will draw a full-body bird.

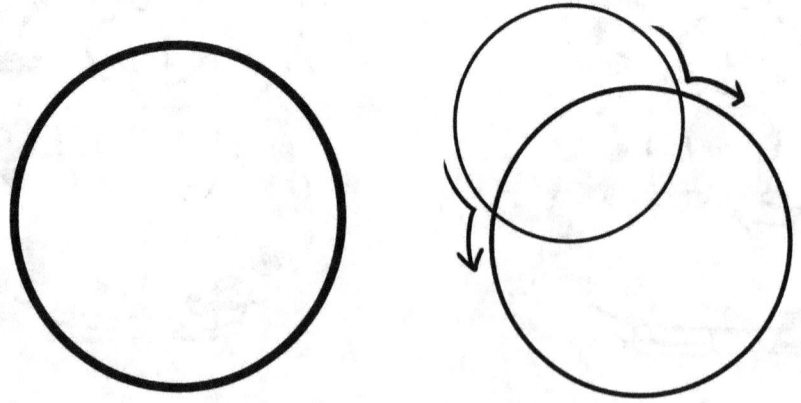

We will start a simple circle for the first bird.
Place a much smaller circle on top of the first one.
The smaller circle would be the head and the bigger one would be the body.

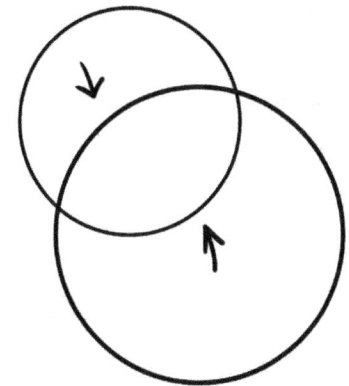 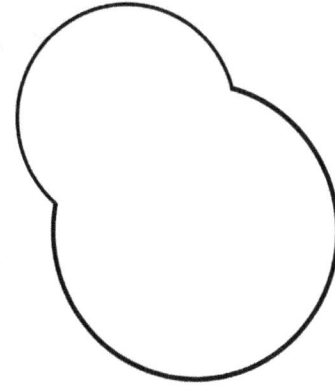

Erase the lines that intersect inside to create a singular shape.

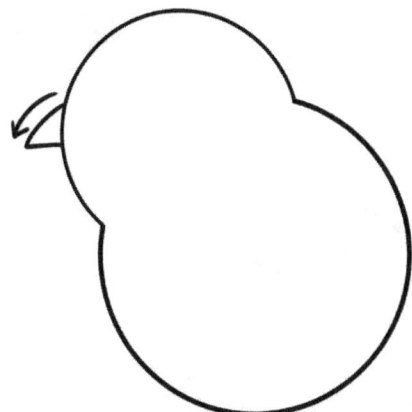 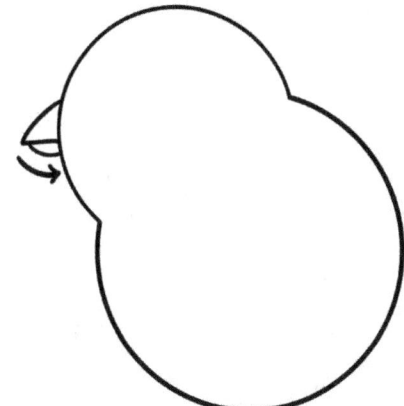

Draw the bird's beak on one side of the head.

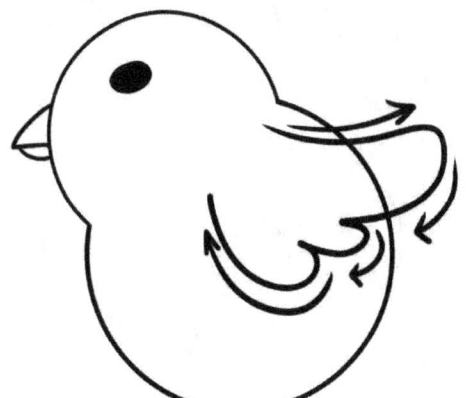 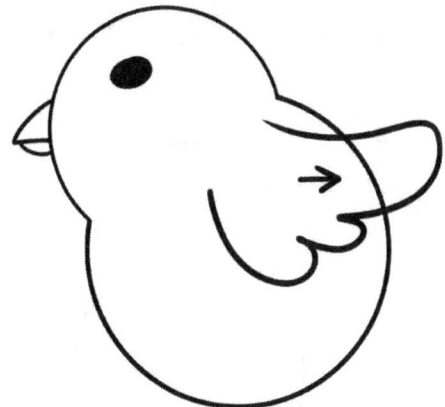

Add the eye and then start drawing the wing.
The wing's curves are shaped like those of a cloud's
but with variation on the length of each curve.
Don't forget to erase the intersecting lines!

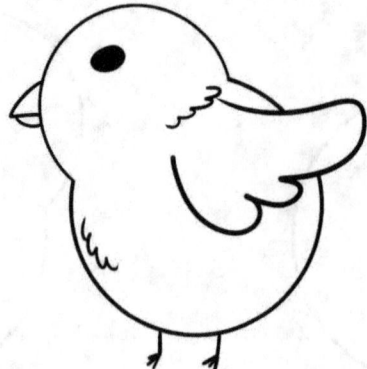

Add the final details like the feet and some more clumps of feathers which are a collection of curves. Your kawaii bird is now done!

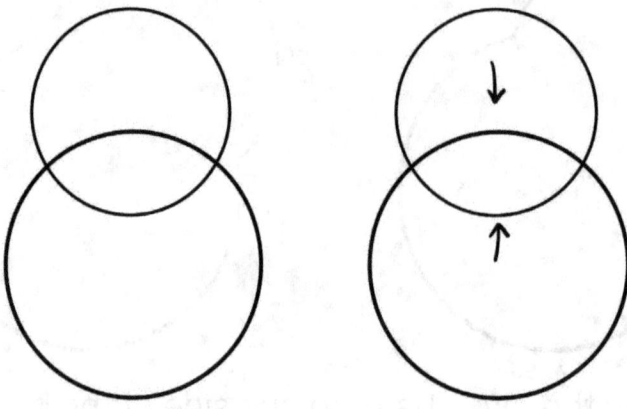

Start with two circles, one smaller than the other.
Place the smaller one on top of the bigger one and erase the intersecting lines.

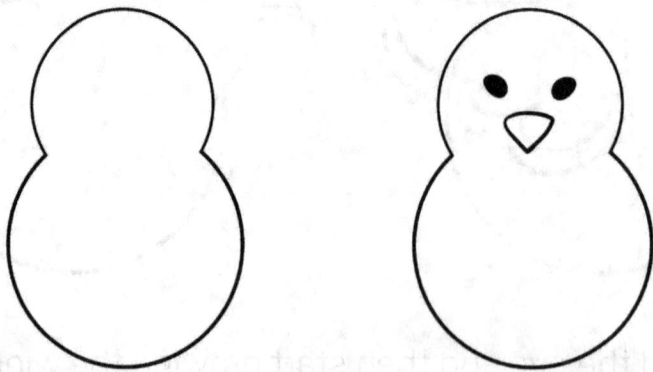

Once you get a singular shape, draw the face of the bird which includes the eyes and the beak.

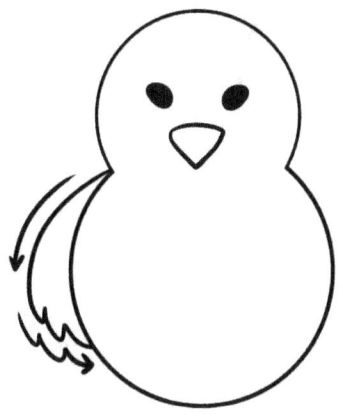

Draw the wing on one side of the body. You can make it smaller and shorter or longer according to your preferences!

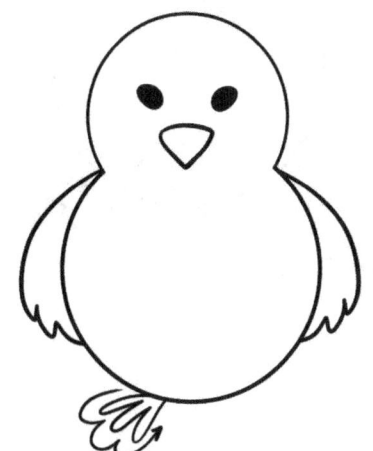

After, draw the other wing on the opposite side.

Then, draw a pair of feet below the body.

Finish it off with details like feathers on the body and on its head!

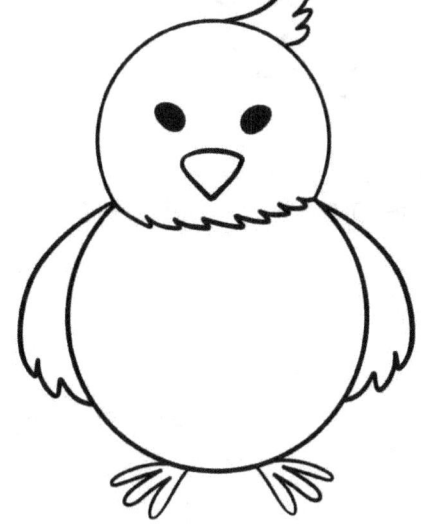

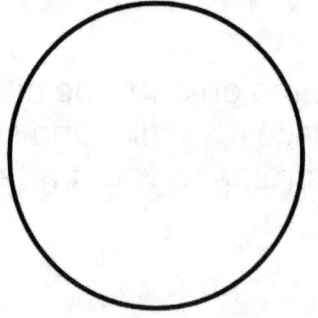 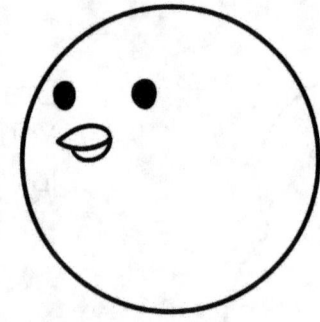

You can even use a simple circle when drawing kawaii birds!
Start with a circle then add the eyes and beak.

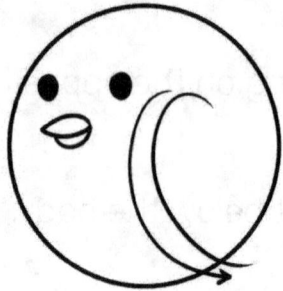 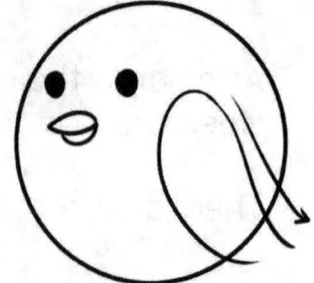 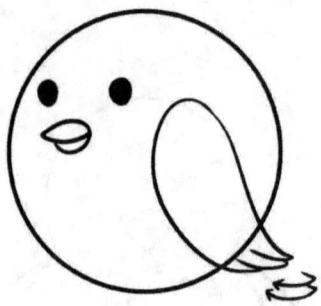

Proceed to drawing the wing using the same techniques
as the previous tutorials.

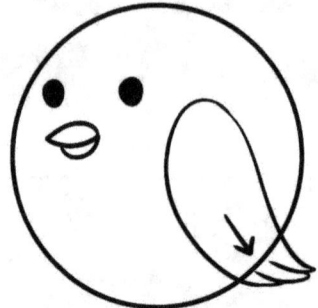 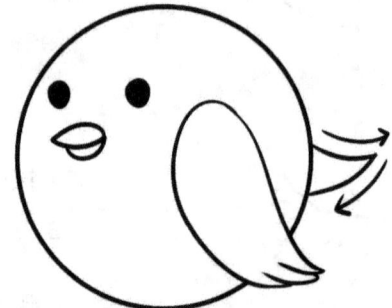

Don't forget to erase the intersecting lines.
You may add a little tail on the side of the body as well!

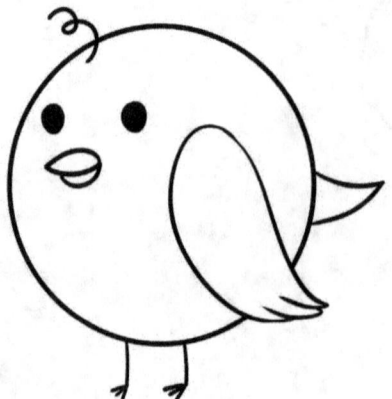

Finally add the feet
and some other
details!

How kawaii!

# KAWAII ANIMALS

Another way of drawing cute animals is by using a simple egg shape!

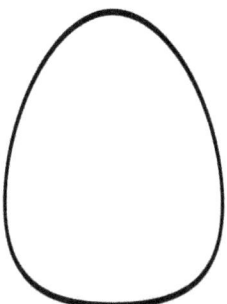

Like the first tutorials, this shape can be used to draw various types of cute animals!
For this example, we will be drawing a cute dog from this egg shape.

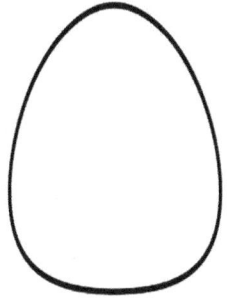

First draw an egg shape.

This will be the whole body of the animal so if you draw a small egg, the animal would be smaller!

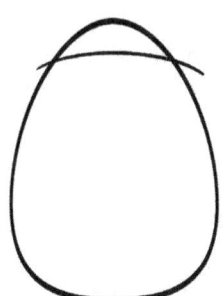

After that, draw a curved line on the top portion of the egg, this will be the guide for the ears.

The higher you draw your guide the shorter the ears would be and vice versa.

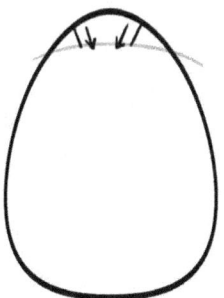

Next step is to draw two lines starting from the top part of the egg going down meeting the guide that we drew.

These would be the ears of our dog.

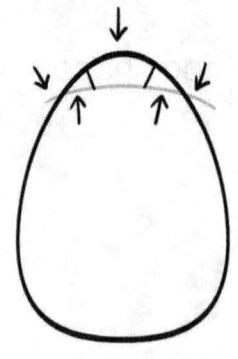

As always, don't forget to erase the intersecting lines!

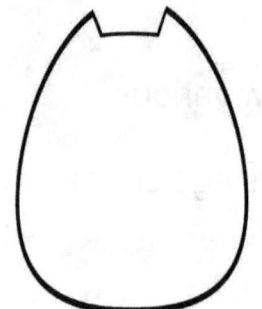 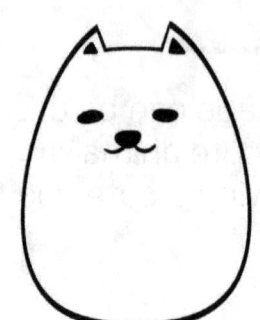

Once you get a singular shape, you can add the facial features like the eyes and the nose!

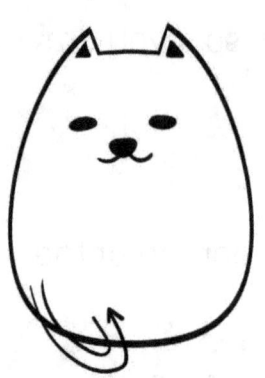 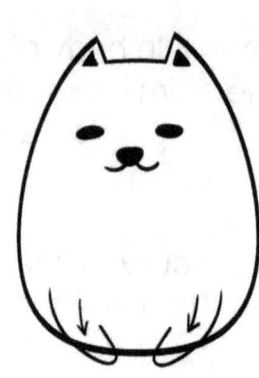

Add the front legs of the dog using curved and rounded lines.

As always, erase the intersecting lines!

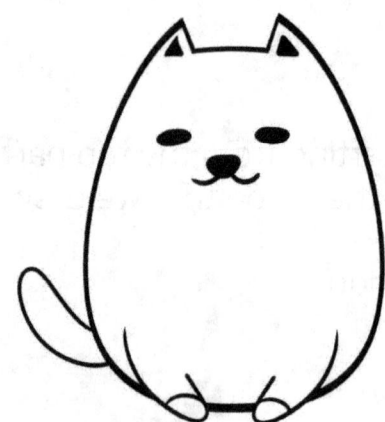

Add the finishing details such as the tail and other details you want to add!
And you're done with our kawaii dog!

# KAWAII ANIMALS
## SEA CREATURES

The next animal chapter would be focusing on kawaii creatures that live in the sea!

## FISH

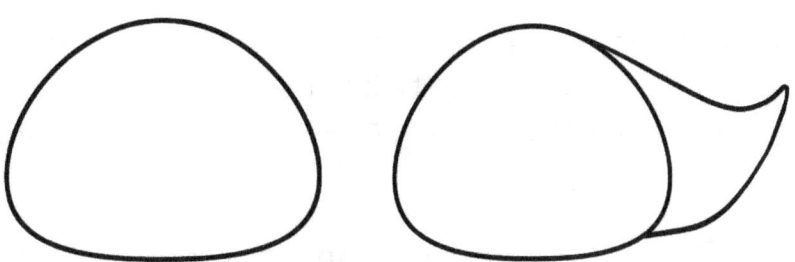

Start with one of the basic shapes
that we have been using to draw kawaii animals.

Draw two curved lines that meet at the end.
You can make them shorter or longer according to your preference.

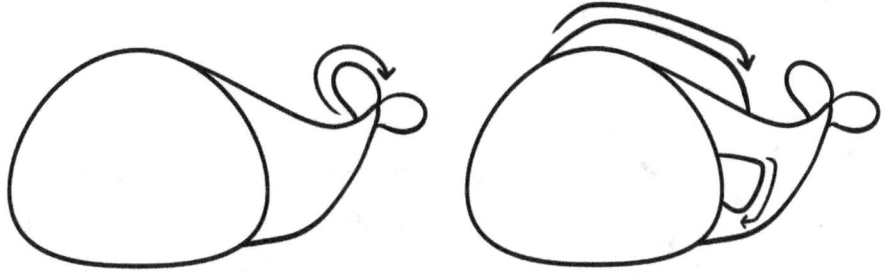

Add the fish's body details such as the tail and the fins.

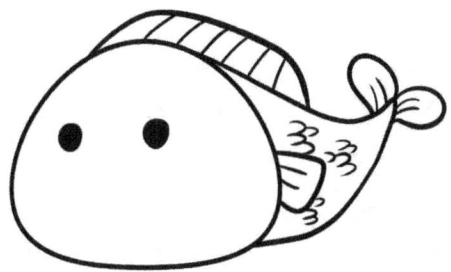

Lastly, add the details of the fish
such as the lines on its fins, tail, and scales!

# OCTOPUS

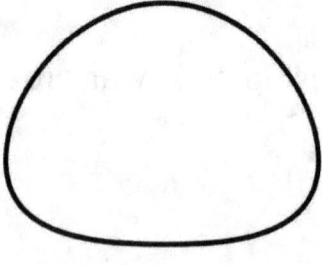
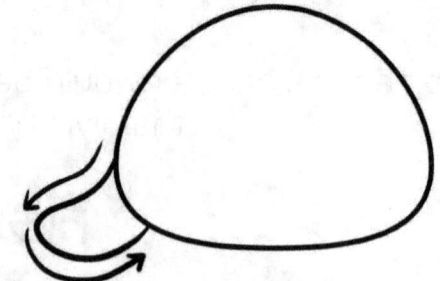

Start with the basic shape then add the octopus' tentacles by drawing rounded curves below the head.
You can draw the tentacles shorter or longer according to your preference.

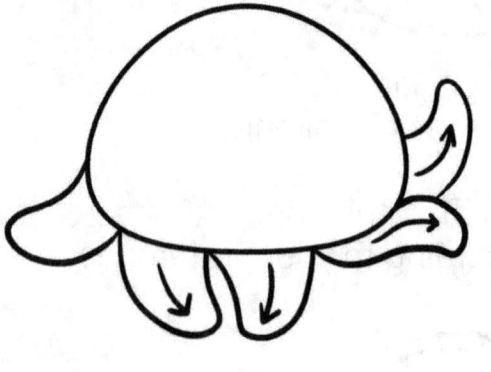

Add the other tentacles. Depending on the view, not all eight tentacles may be visible!

Make sure to draw the tentacles in different directions so that the octopus won't look stiff.

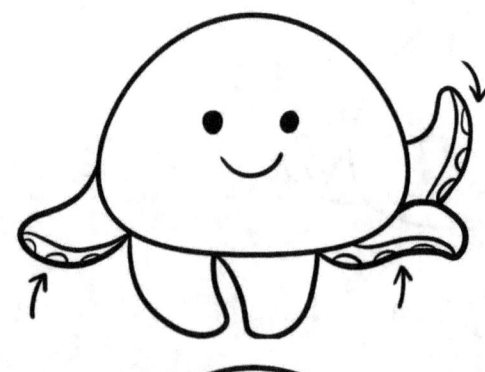

Add the details of the tentacles, remember that the suction cups are placed under each tentacle.

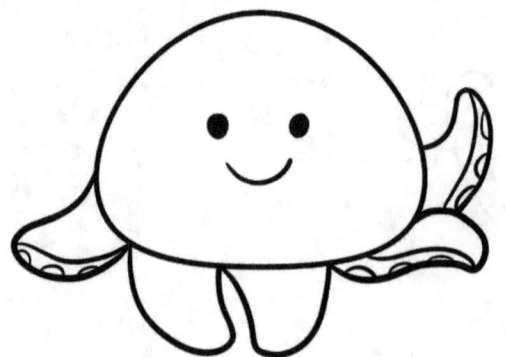

And now you're done!

Feel free to add some details and patterns in the octopus' body.

# TURTLE

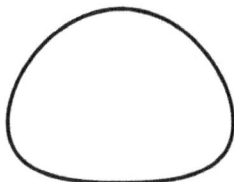 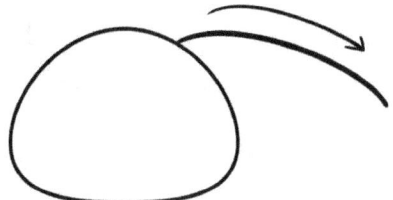 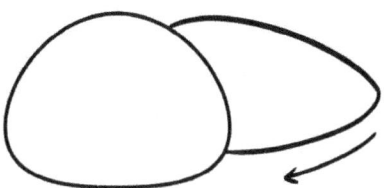

Starting with our basic shape, add two curved lines that have a rounded edge on one side of the head.
This will be the shell of the turtle.

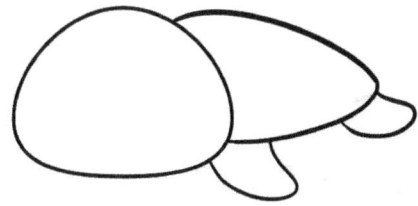

Add rounded curves below the shell. These will be the flippers of the turtle.

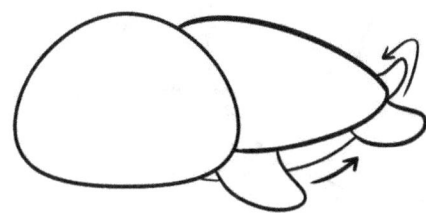

Add more curves to the turtle's body such as its tail and the lining below its shell.

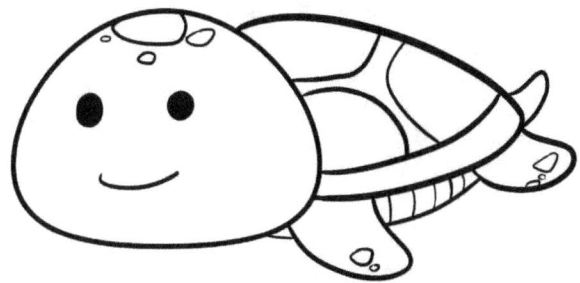

Finally, add the details on its head, flippers and shell.

You're done!

# SHARK

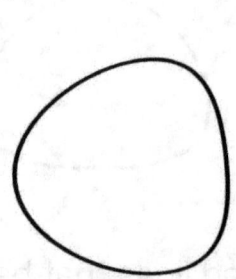 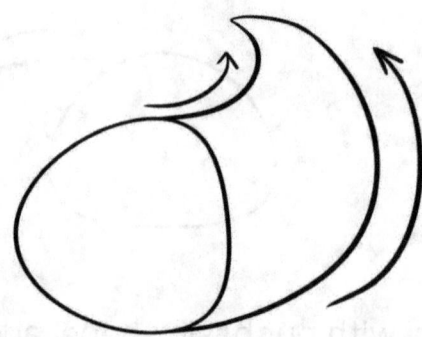

Starting with our basic shape, add two curved lines that will form the shark's body.

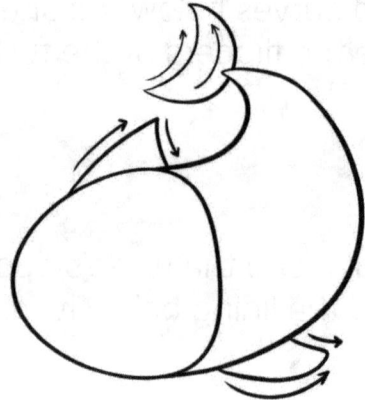 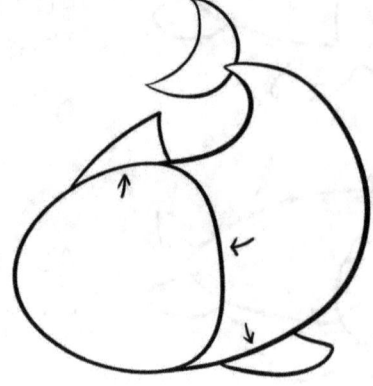

Add more of the shark's body parts such as the fins and tail. Erase the parts where the lines overlap.

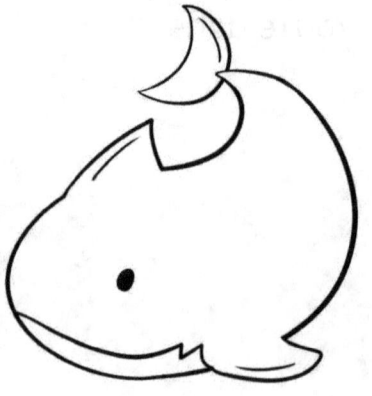

Lastly, add the details that will complete the shark's body.

And you're done!

# WHALE

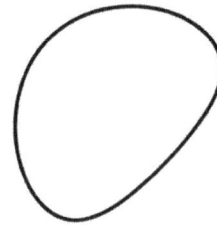 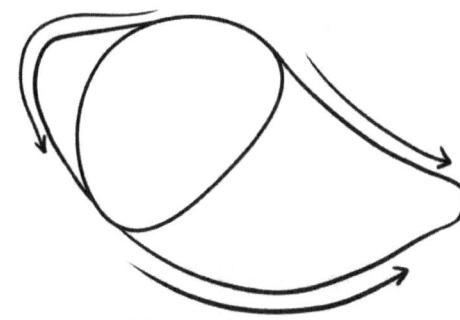

Start with the basic shape and add a curved line on both sides of it, one which is pointed and short which will be part of the head and the other longer which would be the body of the whale.

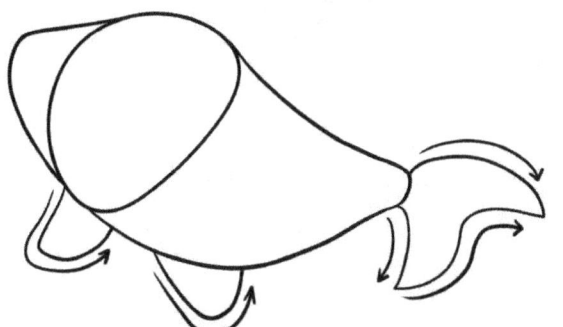 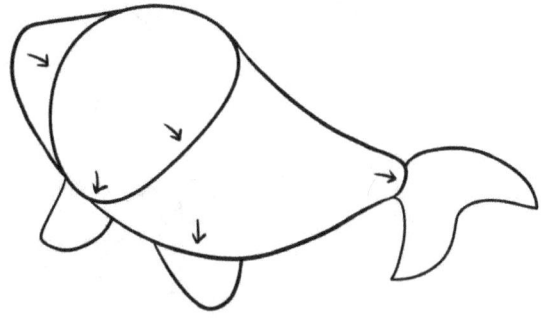

Add the fins and tails of the whale.
Erase the overlapping lines.

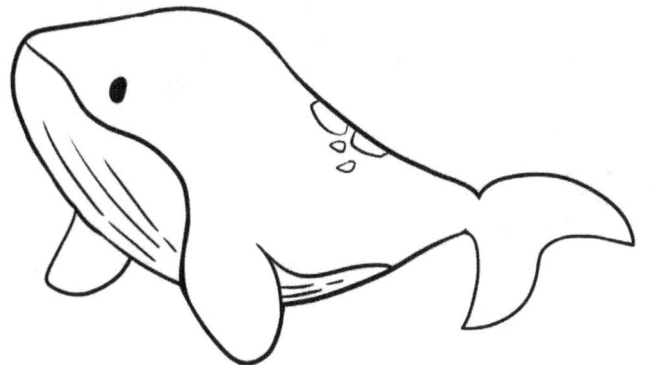

Add the details on the whale's body.

You're done!

# DOLPHIN

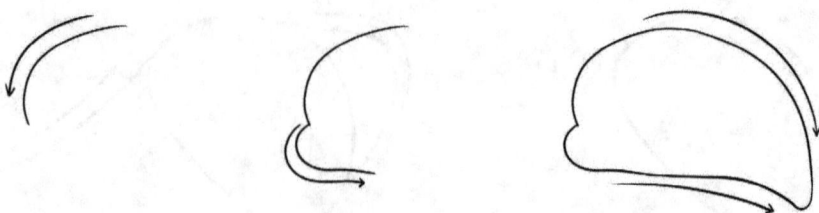

A dolphin's head is a bit different so we won't be using the basic shape that we have been using so far.
The forehead of the dolphin is prominent and they have pointed mouths.

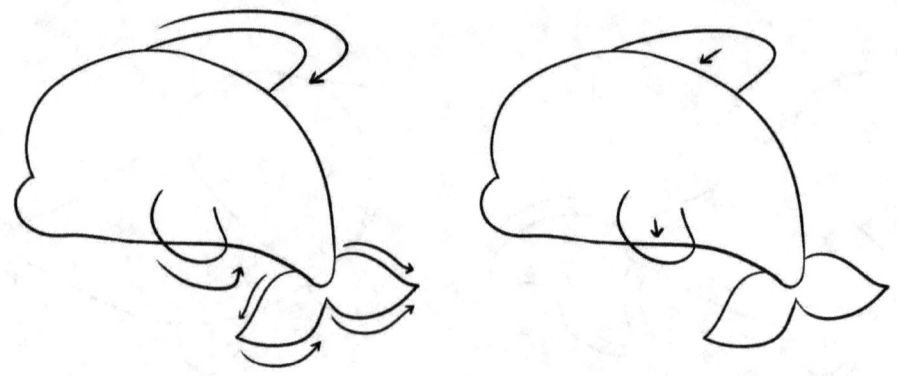

Add the fins and the tail of the dolphin.
Make sure to erase the overlapping lines as well.

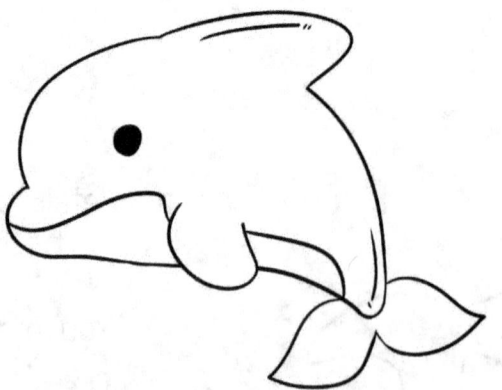

Add the final details to finish your kawaii dolphin and you're done!

# KAWAII ANIMALS
## TALL ANIMALS

## LLAMA

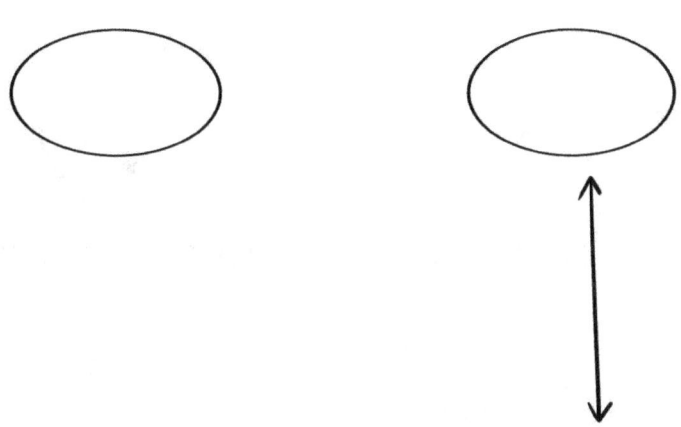

Start with one of the basic shapes.
Since llamas have long necks, we need to determine its length.
Use a guideline to help you in drawing the neck.

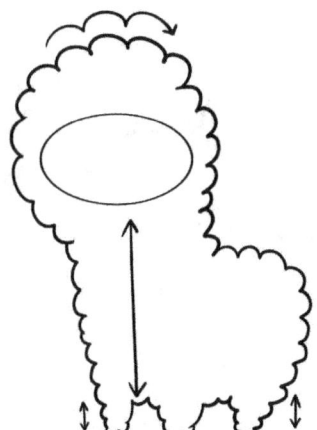

Following the guideline, draw the body of the llama using cloud-like curves since they have fluffy wool! Go around the llama's head and draw short legs.

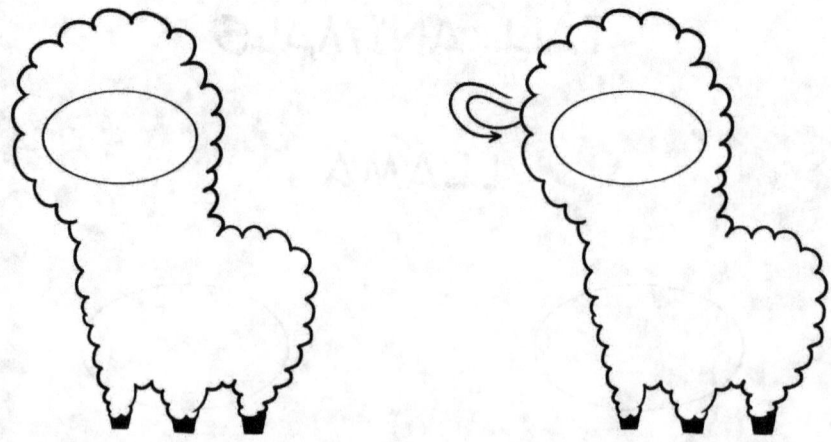

Add the details such as the hooves and the ears.

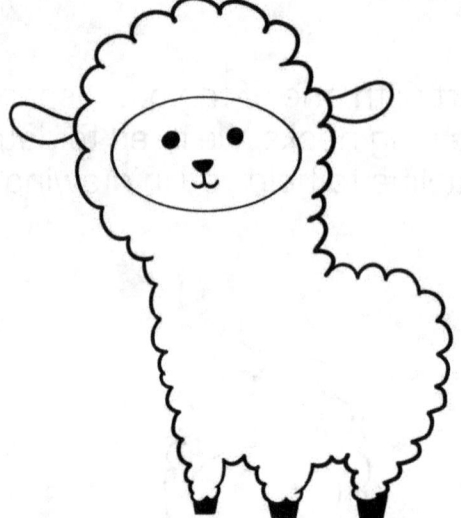

Don't forget to add a kawaii face on the llama and you are done!

# GIRAFFE

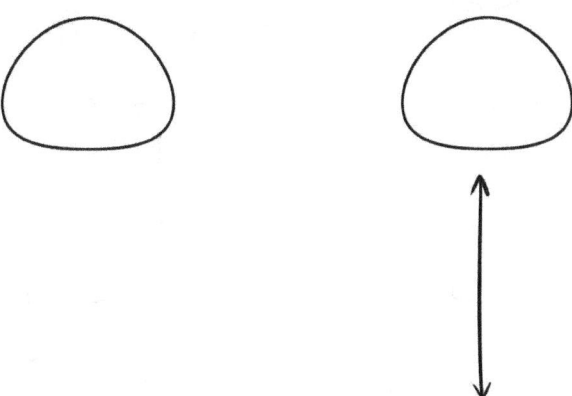

Like what we did on the llama, start with a basic shape and a guideline to help you with the neck.

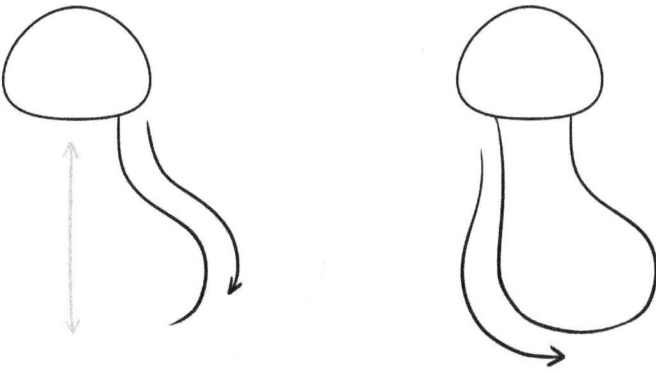

Draw the giraffe's body, make sure that it is rounded especially at the edge.

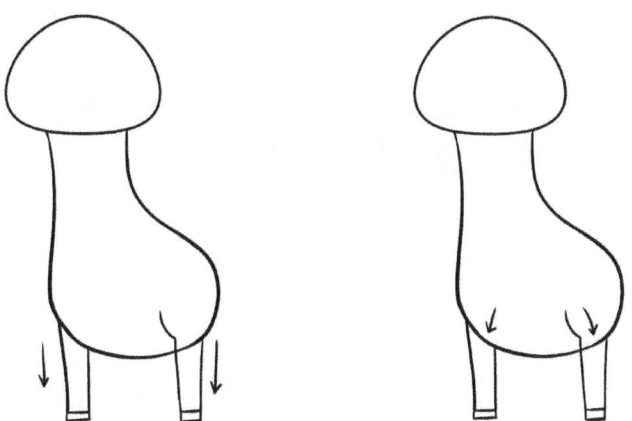

Draw the legs of the giraffe using straight lines.
Add hooves to each of the legs as well.
Don't forget to erase any overlapping lines.

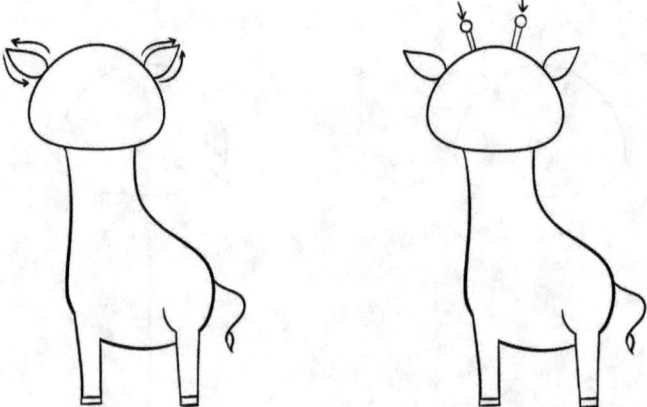

Add the other body parts such as the ears, tail, and the ossicones of the giraffe which are actually horns.

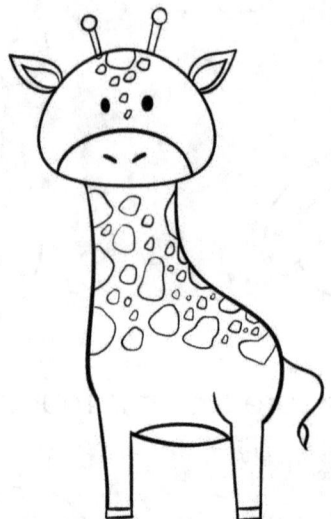

Lastly, add the face of the giraffe as well as the distinct markings in the giraffe's body.

# OSTRICH

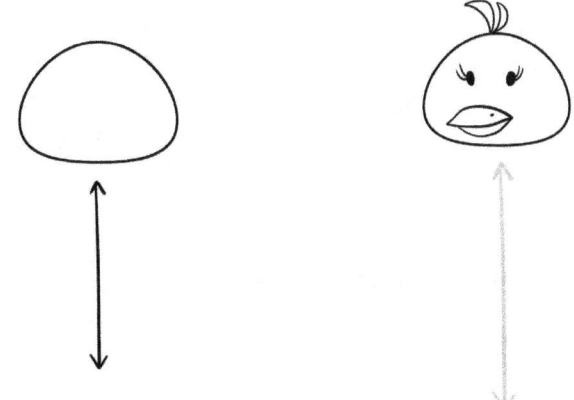

The same process goes for the ostrich.
Start with a basic shape and the guideline.

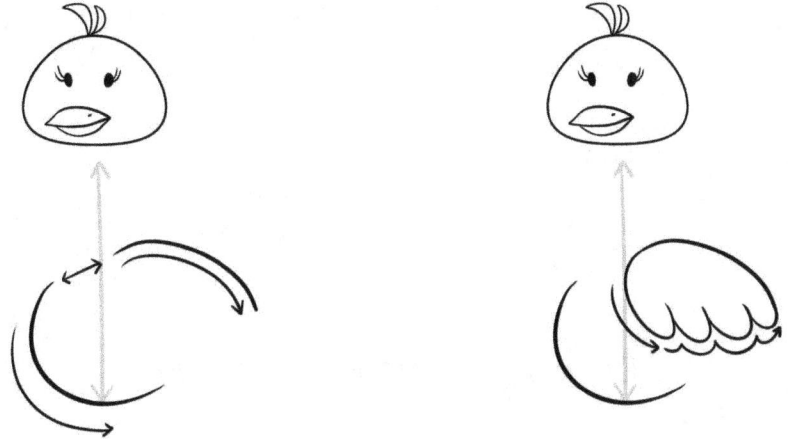

Use curved lines to draw the ostrich's body and wing.

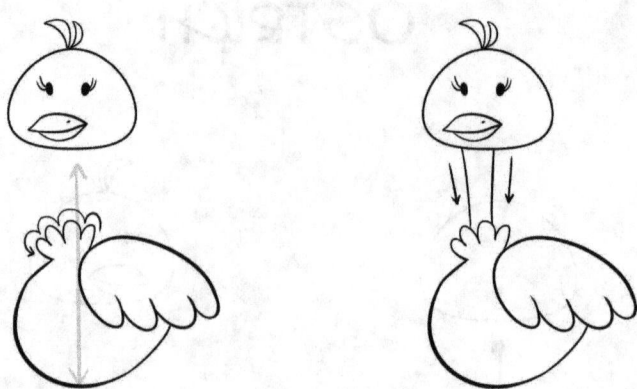

Draw the neck of the ostrich and connect it to the body.

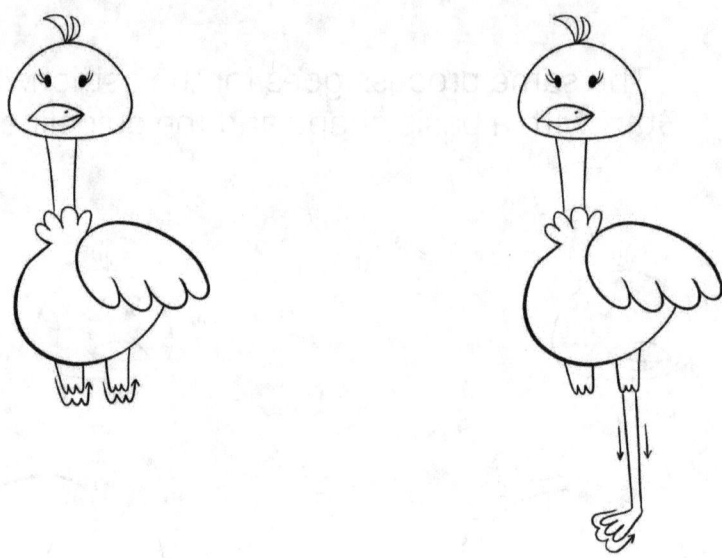

Draw a pair of long legs as well.

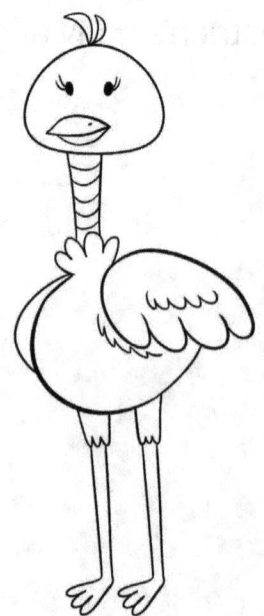

Draw the final details and you are done with your kawaii ostrich!

# KAWAII PLANTS

The next tutorials would be focused in drawing cute plants!
Drawing plants is easy and only requires very few techniques
and basic shapes.

## LEAVES

The first thing to learn is to draw
the most basic part of the plant which is the leaf!

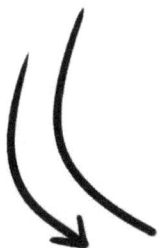 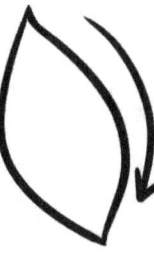

Draw the basic shape of the leaf with two curved lines that meet at the end.
Both ends must be pointed!

 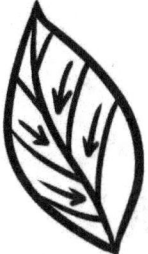

Add the details in the leaf such as the midrib (the middle part of the leaf)
and the veins (the small lines growing from the midrib).

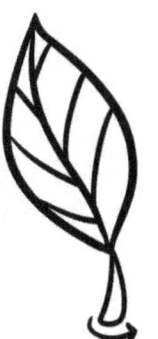

Add the petiole or the stem
at the end of the leaf and
you're done!

 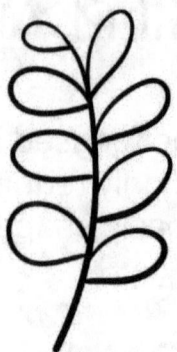 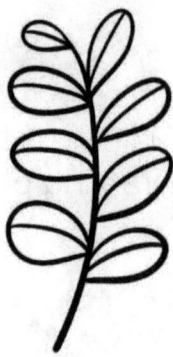

Another leaf shape that's easy to draw is a single stem connected to rounded leaves! Make sure that the leaves become larger when you reach the lower part of the stem.

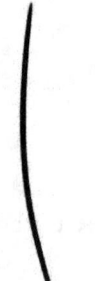 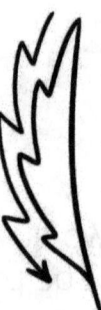 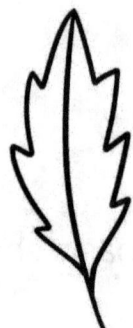

There are also leaves with jagged edges.
We start with the stem then draw
a pair of zigzag lines on both sides of the stem.

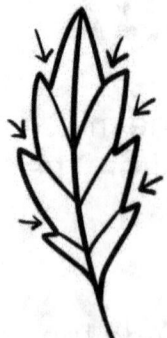 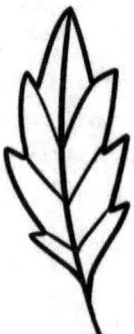

Add the veins of the leaf by connecting it to every edge formed by the zigzag lines. And you're done!

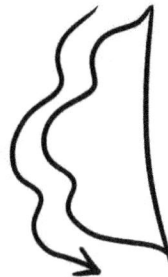 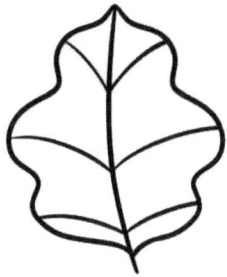

The same process is followed
when working on leaves with wavy edges!

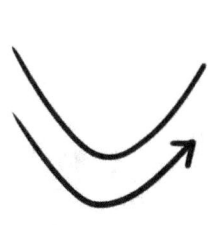 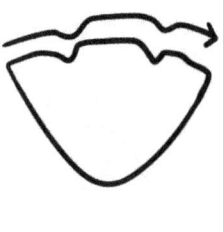 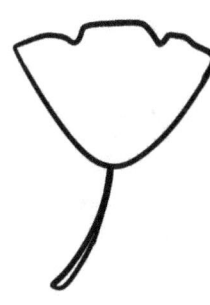

Some leaves have a cup-like shape!
You can add an irregular pattern for its edge too.

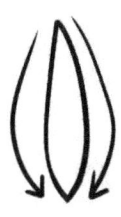 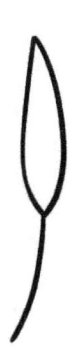 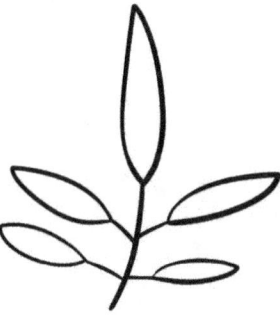

Some plants have wide gaps between the leaves like this one.
You can draw a variation of leaf size as well.

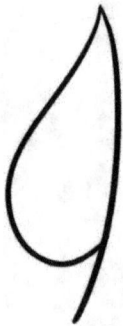 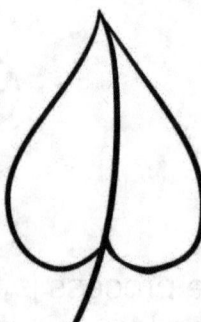 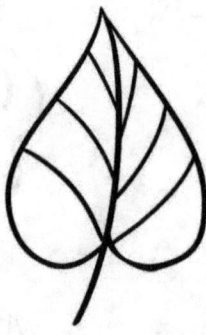

Some leaves are heart-shaped as well!
The same process is used to draw this.

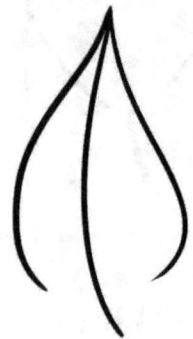 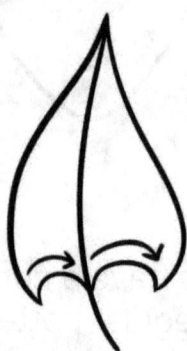 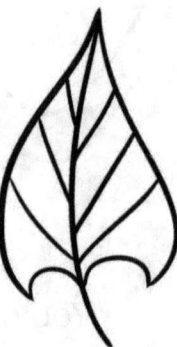

You can add more details to make the leaf shape unique as well!

# KAWAII PLANTS
## FLOWERS

Another fun thing to draw is flowers!
You can draw various shapes
to make each flower a lot more unique!
In this tutorial, we are going to cover the most common flowers!

## ROSEBUD

 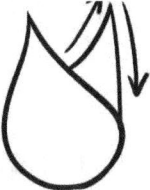

Start by drawing the base petals
using leaf shapes that overlap with one another.
Make sure that the first petal is rounded at the bottom.

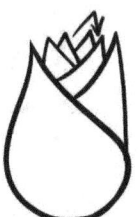 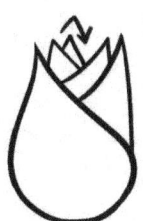 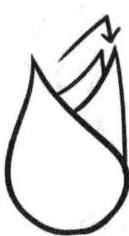 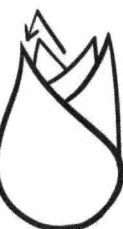

Continue to draw more overlapping petals on top of one another
to create an illusion of a blooming rose!

Finally, add more details like the leaves and the stem to complete the rosebud and you're done!

# ROSE

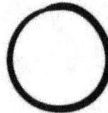 

Start with a small circle then add some curved lines inside it. This would be the bud inside in top view.

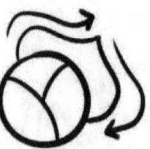 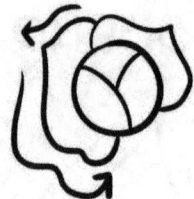 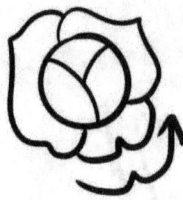

Add three petals outside of the circle by drawing a variation of waved and curved lines. Make sure to overlap one petal with another to create the illusion of layered petals.

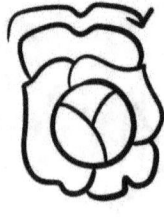 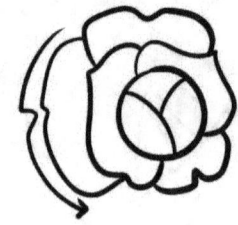 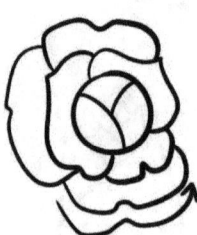 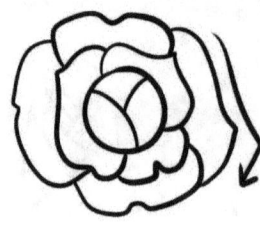

Add three petals outside of the circle by drawing a variation of waved and curved lines. Make sure to overlap one petal with another to create the illusion of layered petals.

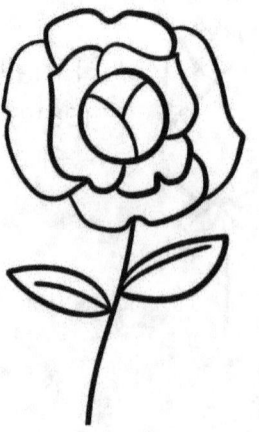

Add the final details like the leaves and the stem of the flower and now you're done drawing your rose!

# DAISY

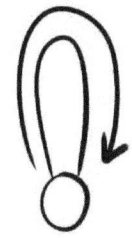

O

To start drawing a daisy, start with a small circle then draw a long and narrow petal that is rounded at the end.

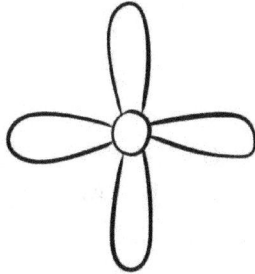 

Add more petals until you reach up to a total of eight petals.

Add some small details so that your daisy won't look plain!

  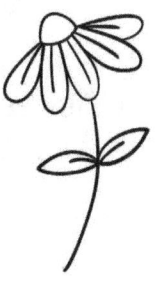

Another version of a daisy is a lazy daisy!
Start by a cup-like shaped head, this is where the petals of the flowers are attached.
Draw the petals as if they are facing down, lastly add the details such as the leaves and stem.

# TULIP

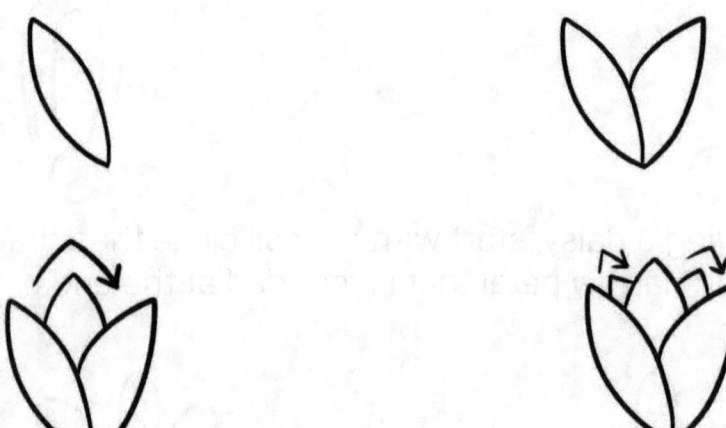

To start with a tulip, follow the same process as in drawing a rosebud. The only difference is that the tulip's petals don't have much curves compared to a rose.
There is also a petal at the center of the first two overlapping petals.

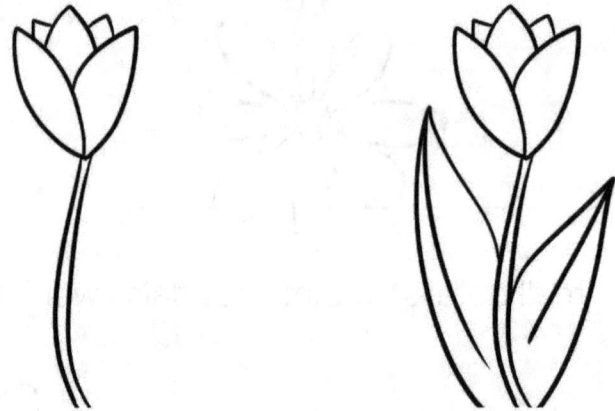

Add the rest of the details to complete the drawing.
Tulips' leaves are long and slender compared to other flowers!

# SUNFLOWER

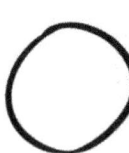 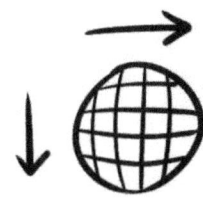

To start drawing a sunflower, start with a circle then draw a grid pattern inside of it using vertical and horizontal lines that intersect with each other.

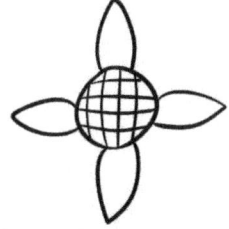 

Add pointed petals to the circle by numbers.
When the flower already has a lot of petals then it's good to go!

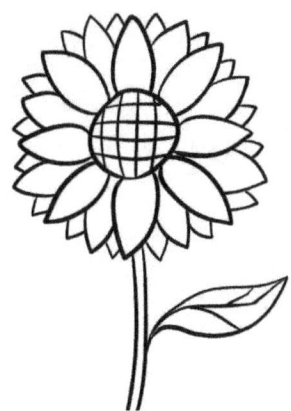

# CHERRY BLOSSOM

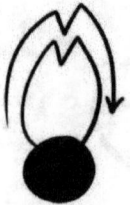

Cherry blossoms are small flowers that grow on the branches
of a cherry blossom tree.
To start drawing it, draw a circle then add a short petal with
a small gap on its edge.

Continue to draw the petals until you reach five.
Draw the details to complete the flower.

# KAWAII PLANTS
## HOUSE PLANTS

House plants have recently become popular because they're easy to take care and are cute!
Drawing house plants is easy since it's basically drawing leaves, stems, and flowers all together in a pot!

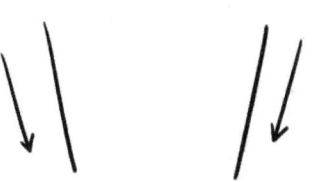 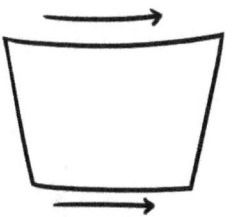

The first thing to draw is the pot itself!
The most common shape for a plant pot is a simple square shape, the top must be a bit curved to make it look rounded!
You can draw whichever shape you want your pot to be, some people use bottles, mugs, and even glass as their plant's pot!

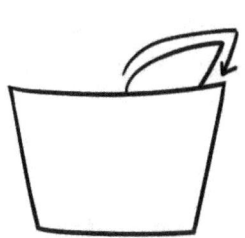 

Draw some short leaves and overlap them with one another to create an illusion of layers.
You can draw as many leaves as you want!

Finally, add designs to your potted plant to make it look a lot livelier!
You can design the pot however you want it!

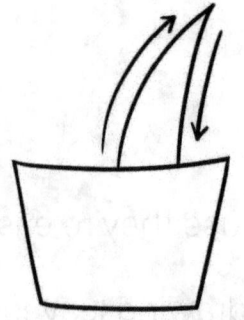 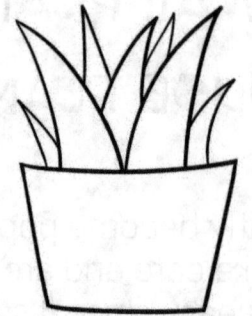 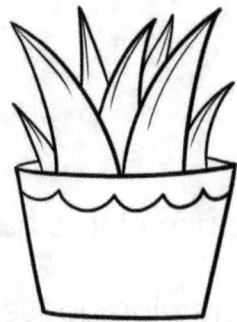

Another style of drawing a house plant
is drawing the leaves tall and sharp like this!
The same process and technique were applied as the first one.

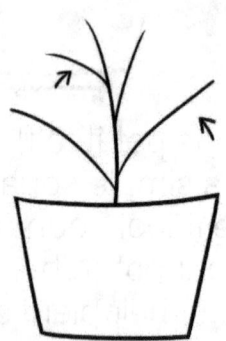 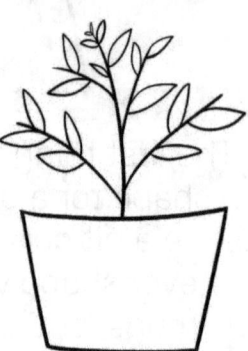

You can also draw a plant with multiple stems and short leaves. Remember that the stems at the bottom are longer than those which are on top.
This variation adds dimension to your plant.

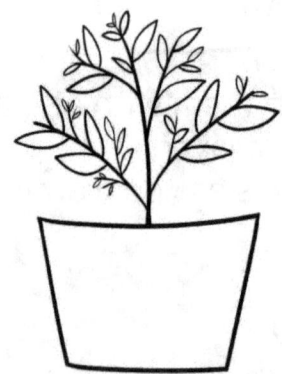 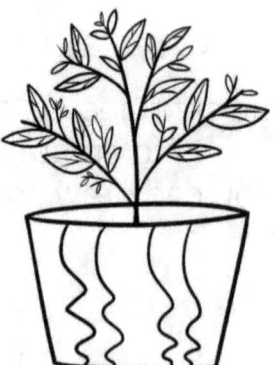

Adding smaller stems in between gaps can create a livelier houseplant!
Don't forget to add the details on the leaves and pot.

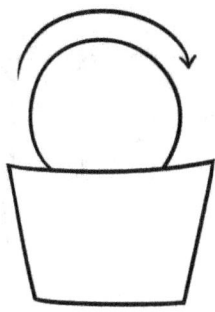 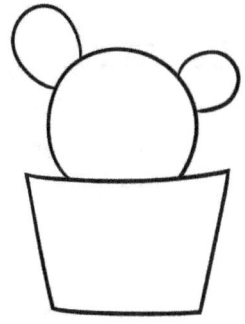

Another popular type of houseplant is cacti!
They have different shapes and sizes and their appearance varies. In this example, we have a rounded cactus with smaller pads attached to it.

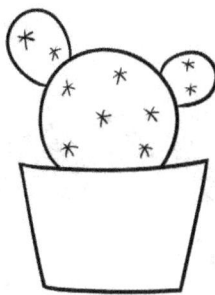 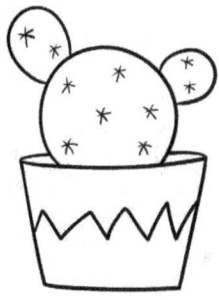

Add the spines of the cactus and the design to the pot!

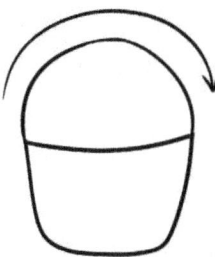 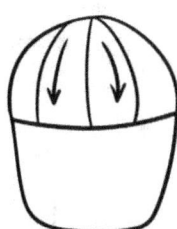

Another common cactus shape is a rounded one.
Draw a curved line over the pot and draw some lines from the top of the curve going down to meet the pot.

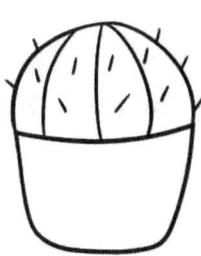 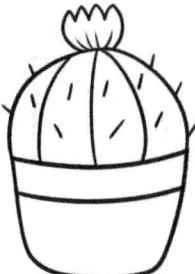

Add the final details such as spines, a simple flower bud on top and the design to the pot as well.

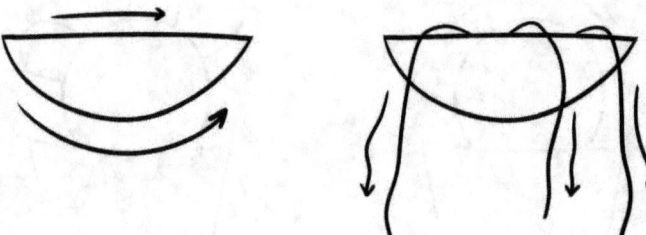

Another common type of a house plant is a hanging one with long stems growing out of the pot.
The pots are usually shaped in shallow-bowl like forms.
Draw the long stems hanging out with wavy lines.

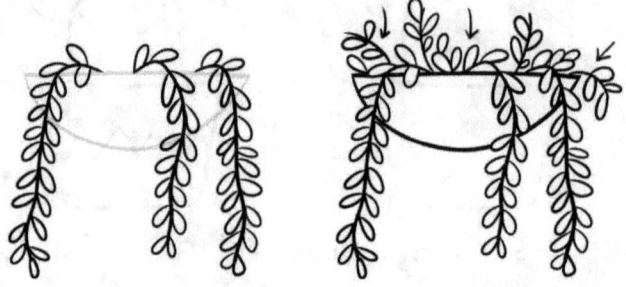

Add rounded leaves on the stem and on the gaps between them to create more dimension.

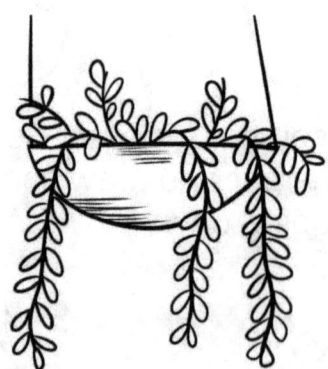

Remember to add in the final details to your plant!

# KAWAII CREATURES
## UNICORN

Unicorns are magical creatures known for their magical horn that grows in their foreheads.
They are usually associated with cute themes like hearts, rainbows, and stars so make sure to get your kawaii on when drawing unicorns!

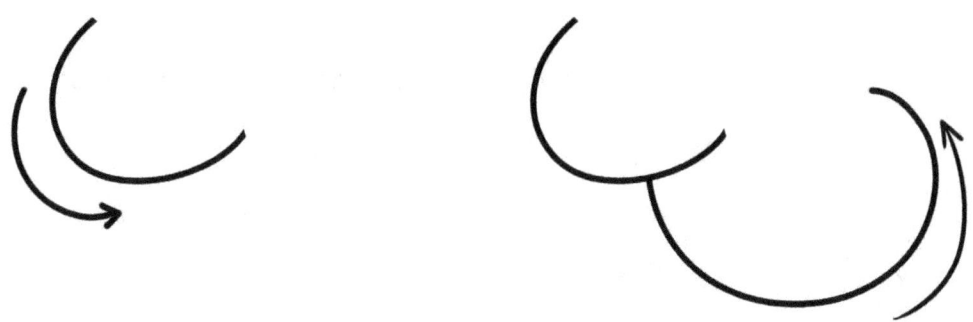

Start drawing the unicorn's body with two rounded shapes, a smaller one for the head and a bigger one for its body.

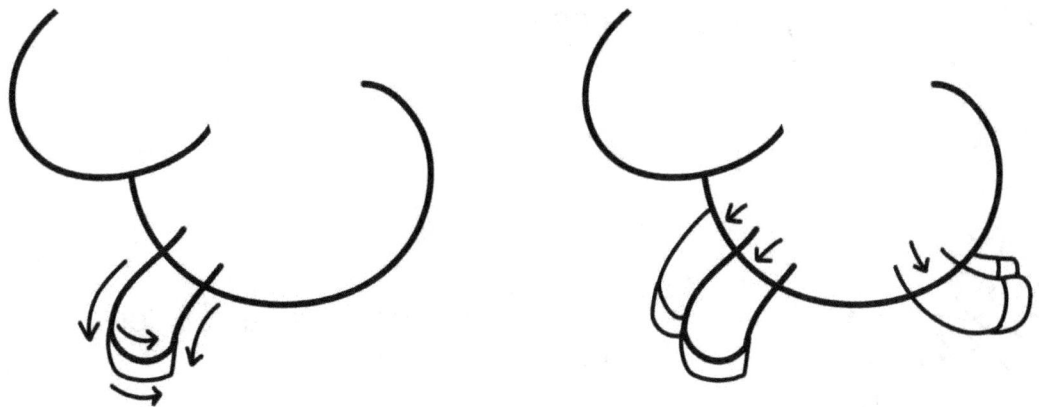

Draw the legs and hooves of the unicorn.
Don't forget to erase any overlapping lines.

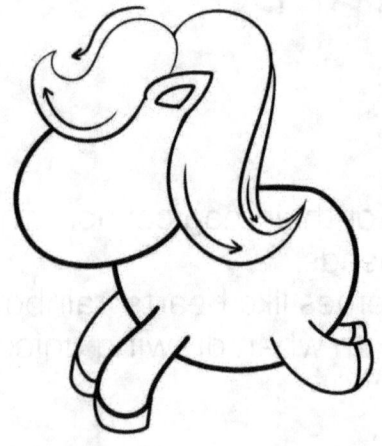 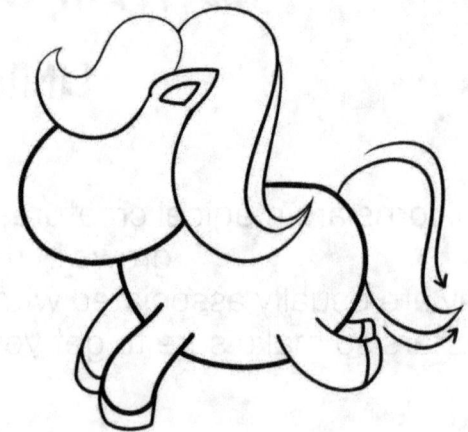

Draw the unicorn's mane and tail using poofy and curvy lines.
Unicorns have fancy hair
so don't be afraid to make it longer!

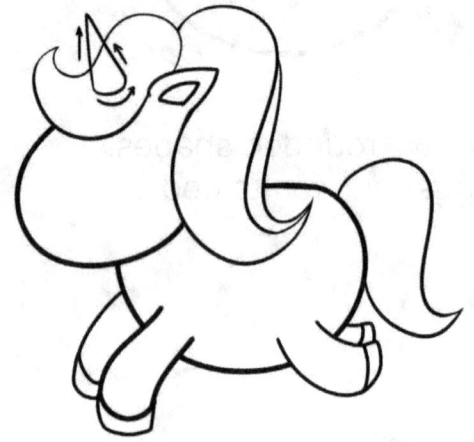

Don't forget about the horn!
It's the most distinguished quality of a unicorn after all.

Place it on its forehead by drawing a cone.

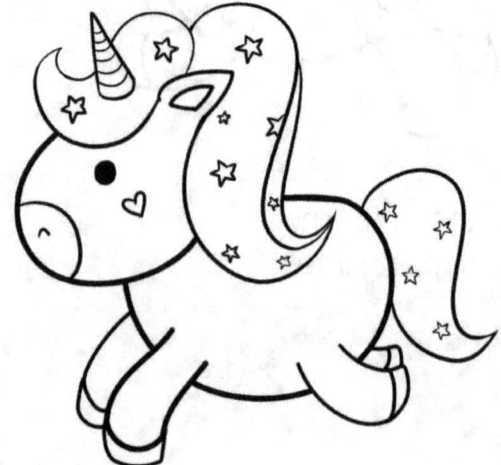

Finish it off with the kawaii designs and details!

Go crazy in adding various shapes like hearts, stars and even rainbows!

Make your unicorn look kawaii!

# KAWAII CREATURES
## MERMAIDS

Mermaids are one of the most popular magical creatures!
They are beautiful humans with a lower body of a fish.
It is easy to draw them since
we're basically combining a chibi and a fish!

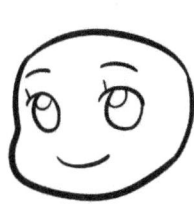 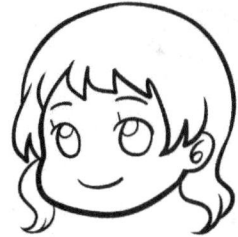

Start off with the first steps of drawing a chibi which are
the head and its details.

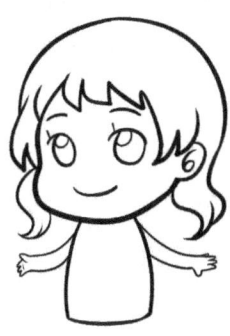 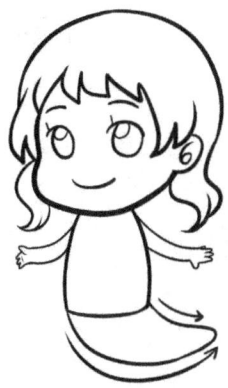

Draw the torso of the mermaid and the tail.
Use the same steps in drawing a fish's body to draw your mermaid's tail.

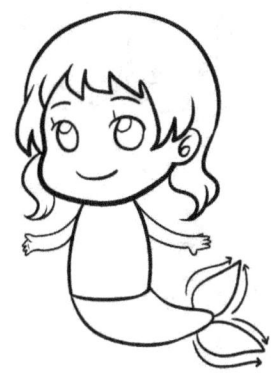

Don't forget to draw the tail as well.

You can draw various shapes of tails to
make your mermaid look more unique.

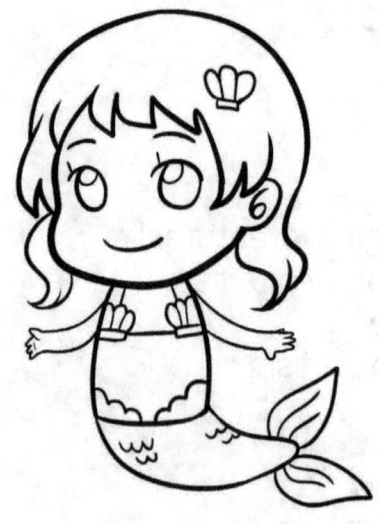

Lastly, add the details of the mermaid such as various accessories, tail details, and other details you want to add.

Your mermaid is done!

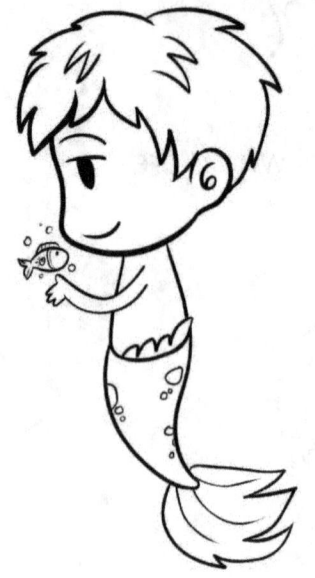

The same steps are used when drawing chibi mermaids facing sidewards!

Remember to add various details and use different tail shapes to make them look unique!

Don't be scared to add a lot of details and accessories!
You can even make the mermaid's ears pointed, draw some clothing, and put on various designs on their hair and body!

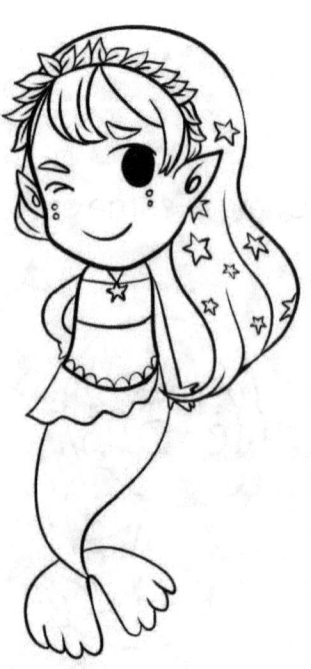

# KAWAII CREATURES
## PEGASUS

Pegasus are magical creatures that are closely related to unicorns because they take after horses too!
The difference is that pegasus have wings!
We will use the same steps as we did when drawing the unicorn.

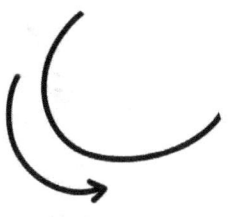 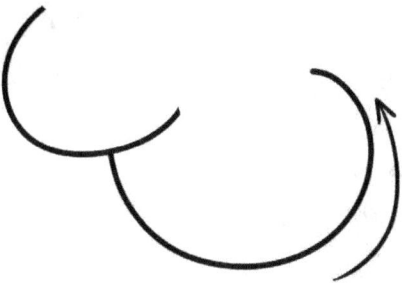

Start drawing the pegasus' body with two rounded shapes, a smaller one for the head and a bigger one for its body.

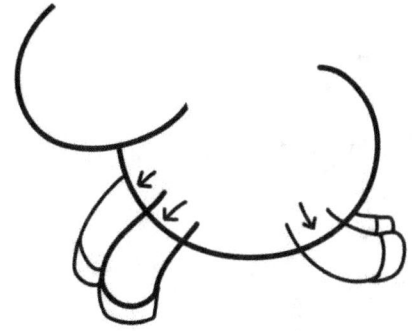

Add the legs and hooves as well.

Don't forget to erase the overlapping lines.

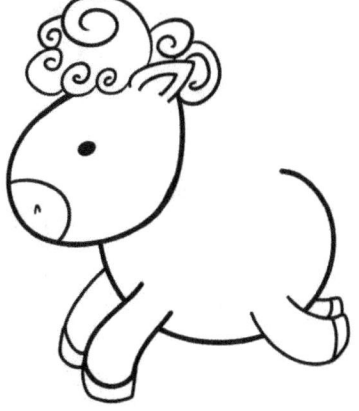

Add the mane of the pegasus. You can style it according to your preference.

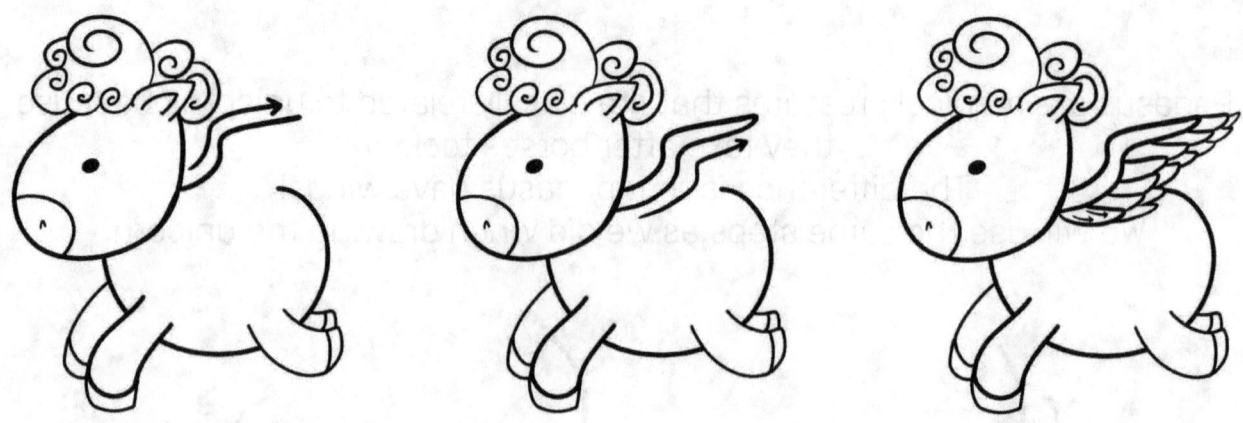

Draw the wings of the pegasus which is its most distinct body feature! You can make it wider or smaller according to your preference!

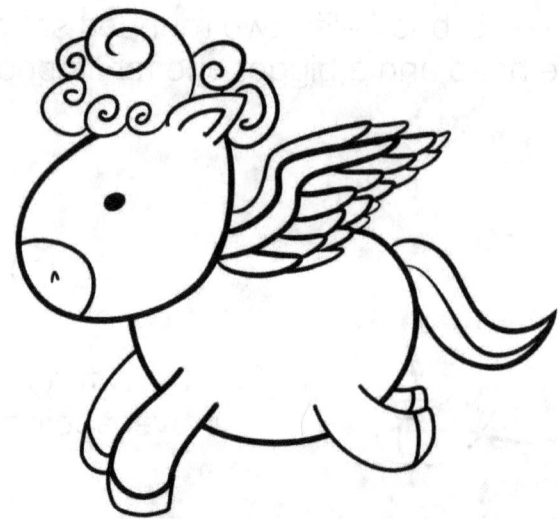

Add the final details to your pegasus and you're done!

# KAWAII CREATURES
## FAIRIES

Fairies are also popular magical creatures.
They are basically human-like creatures with wings and are usually depicted as very close to nature.
Fairies have the same body features as humans, so the same steps in drawing chibis are followed.

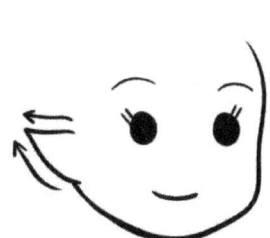 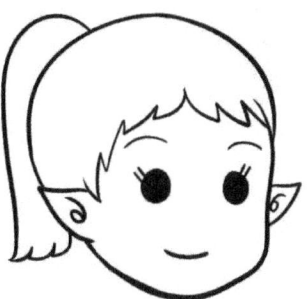

Start with the same steps as you would when drawing a chibi human, but make sure to make the ears pointed.

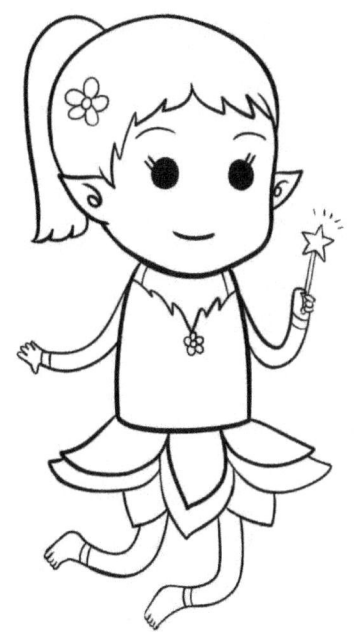

When designing for fairies' clothing make sure to incorporate nature-related themes like flowers and leaves.

Don't forget their wands as well!

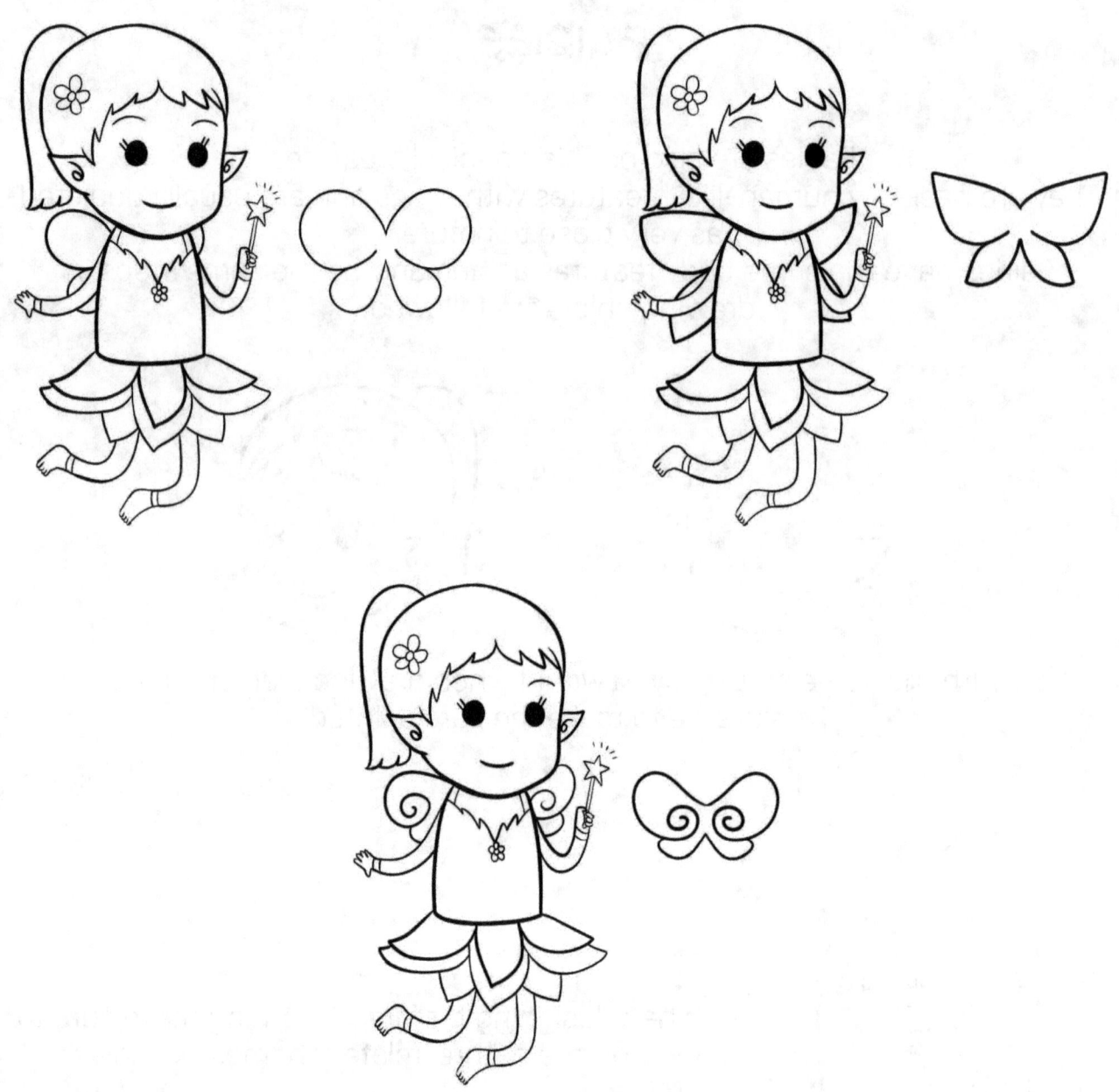

You can choose between a variety of wing shapes!
Make sure to choose one that suits your taste!

# KAWAII CREATURES
## DRAGON

Dragons are known to be ferocious creatures! They're big, scary and they even breathe fire! But for this tutorial, we will make them kawaii!

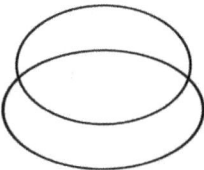 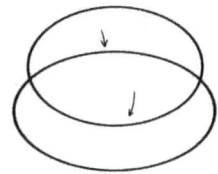 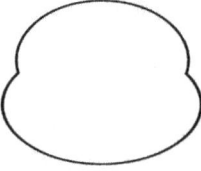

Let's start with the dragon's head by drawing two ovals on top of each other.
One must be bigger than the other.
Remember to erase the overlapping lines so we get one
shape for the dragon's head.

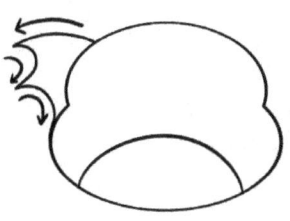

Next, draw the dragon's ears!

They look like bat's wings!
You can also draw them as pointed ones.

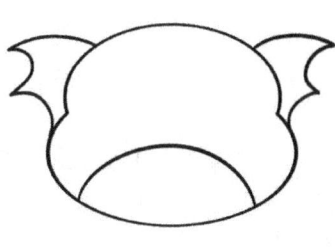 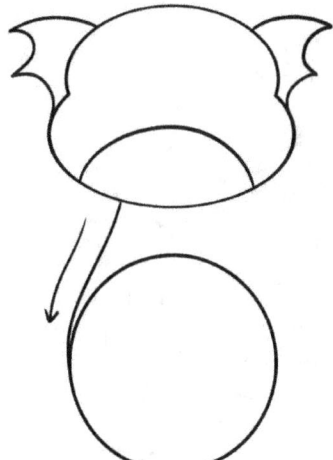

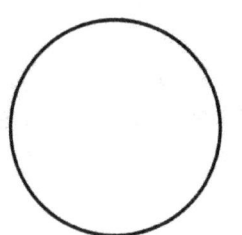

Draw the dragon's belly by drawing a circle below the head. Connect the head and the belly with a slanted line, make sure to do this on both sides.

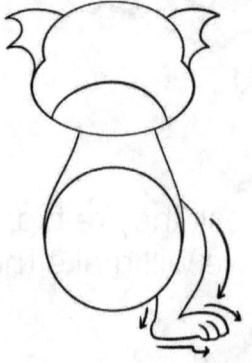
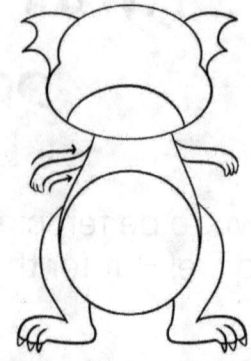

Next to draw are the legs and arms of the dragon.

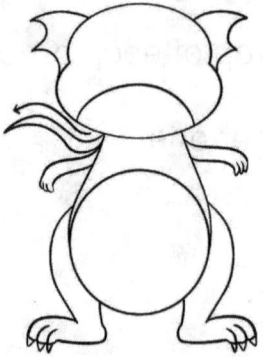
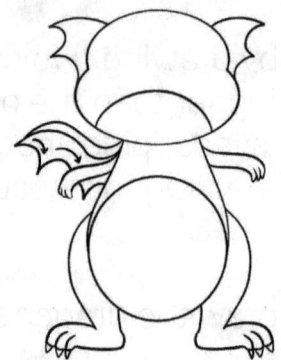
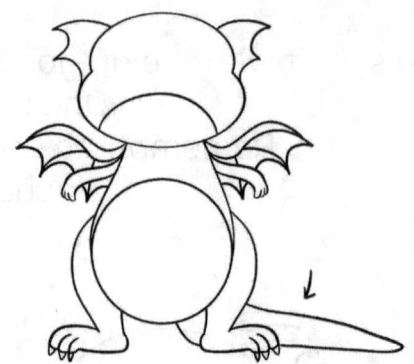

Then draw the wings of the dragon which are a pair of bat-shaped wings! Also draw a big, long tail behind him!

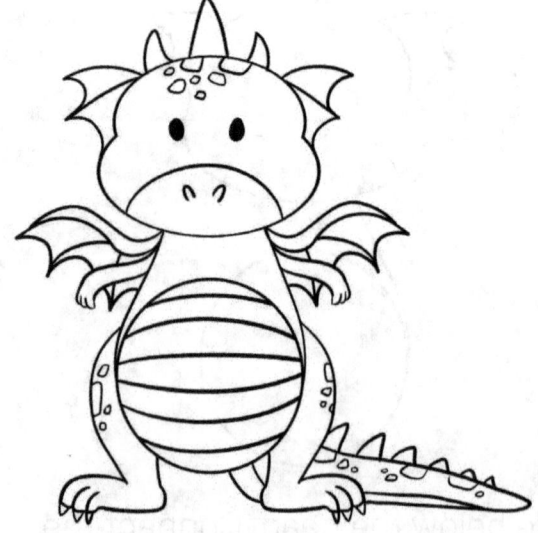

Finally finish off your kawaii dragon by adding details such as skin patterns, horns, and claws!

Make your dragon as cute as possible so that no one would get scared of him!

# KAWAII OBJECTS
## BOY'S THINGS

1. WATCH

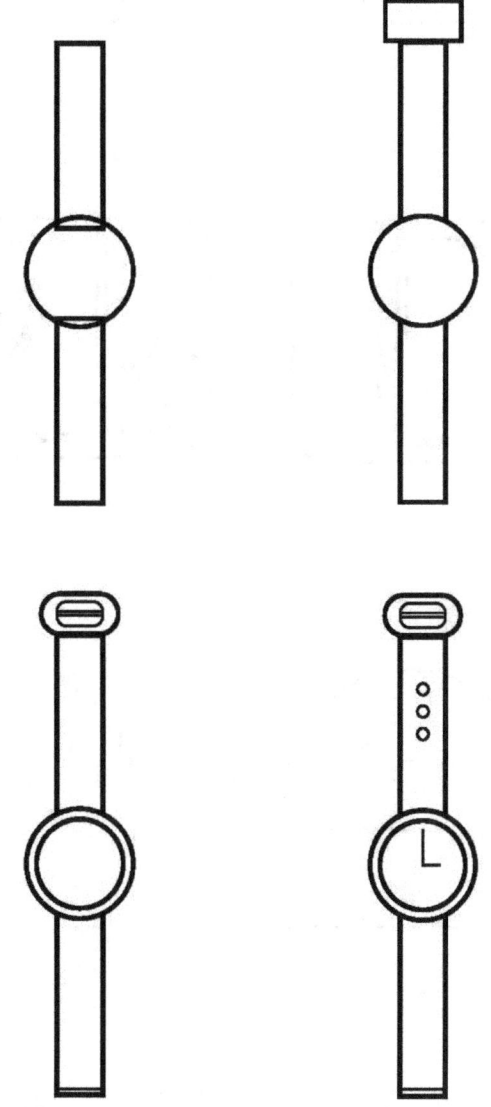

2. GAME CONSOLE

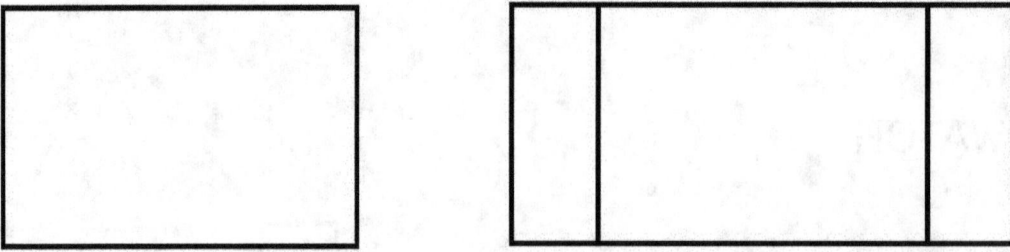

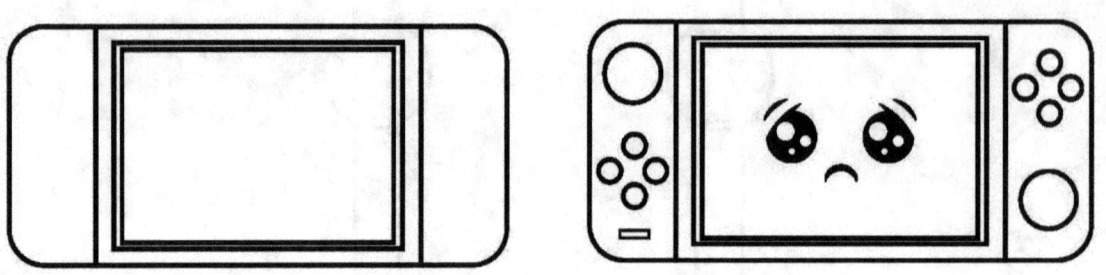

3. BEANIE

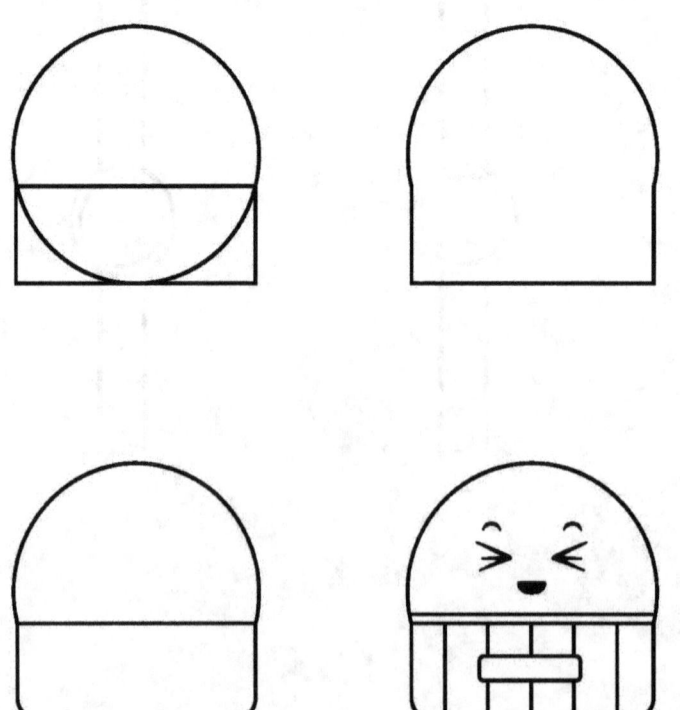

4. BACKPACK

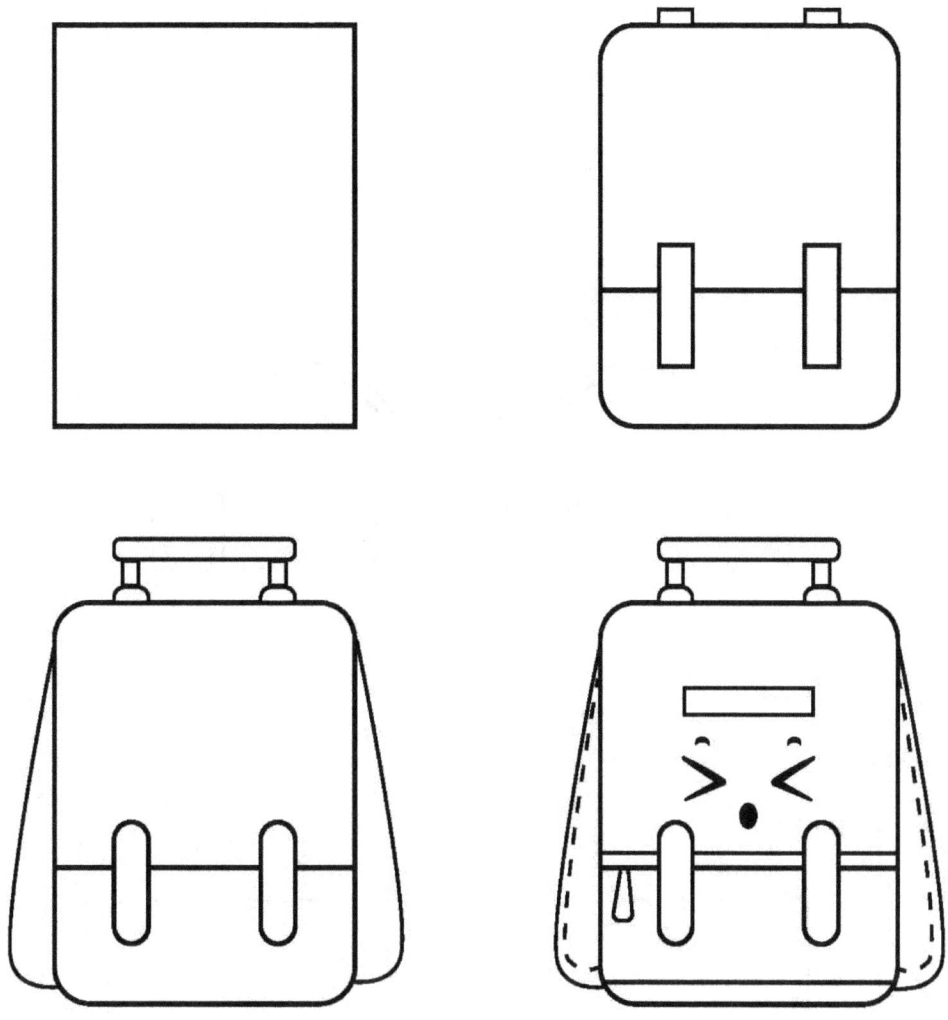

5. HEADPHONES

6. WALLET

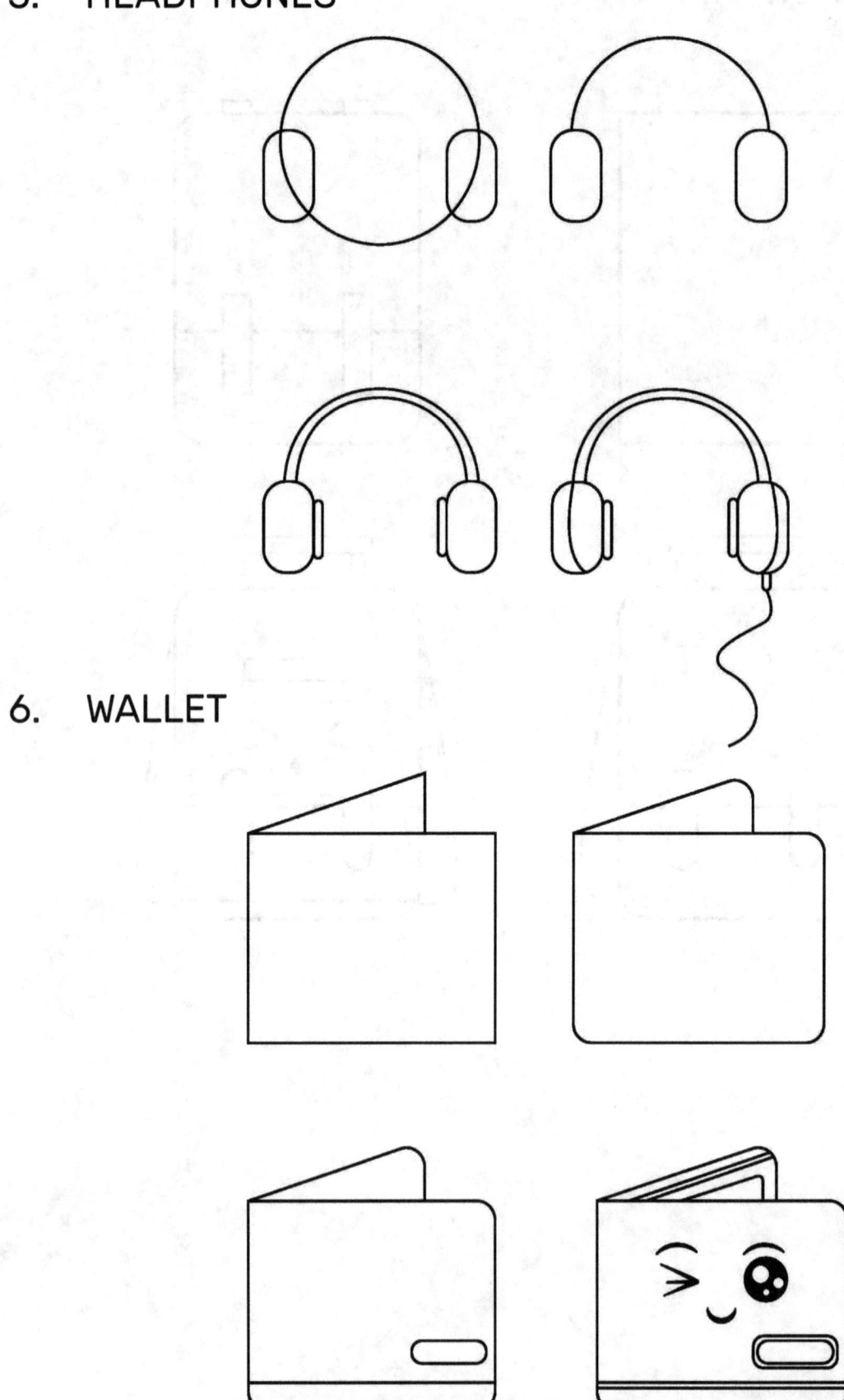

7. WATER TUMBLER

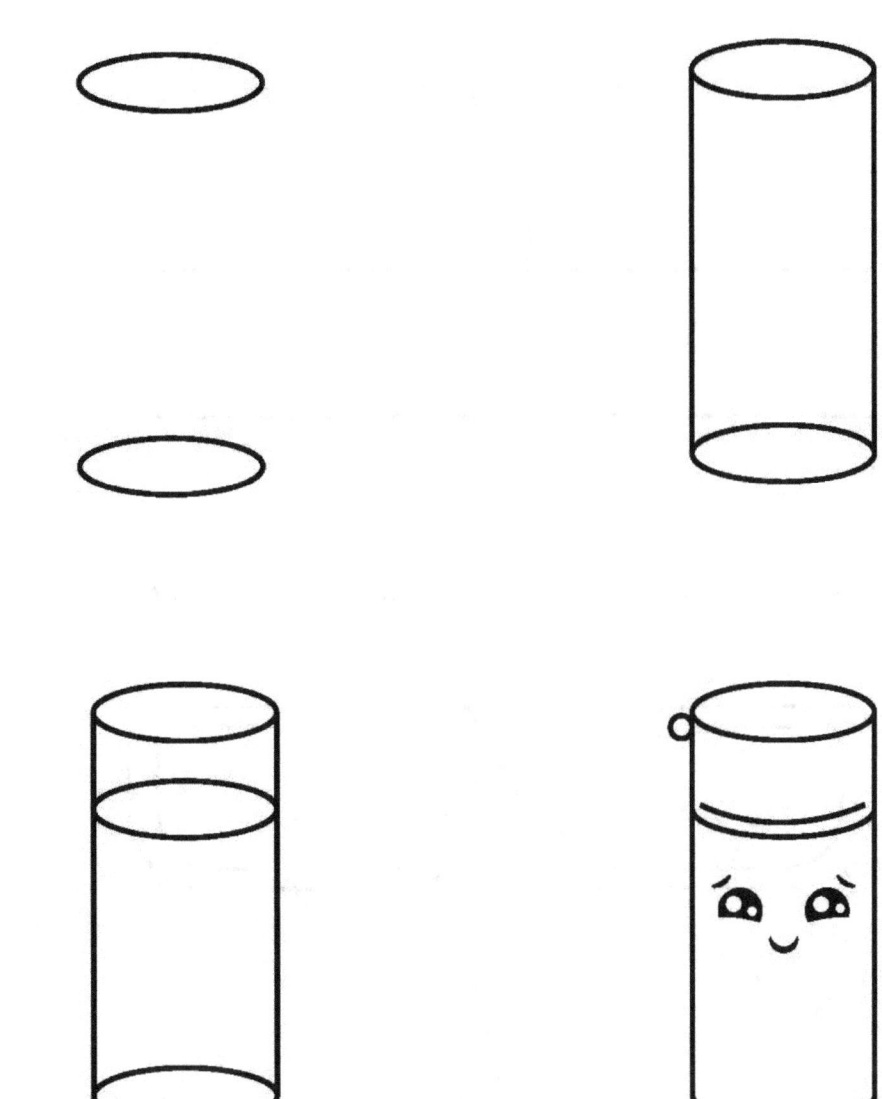

## 8. EYEGLASSES

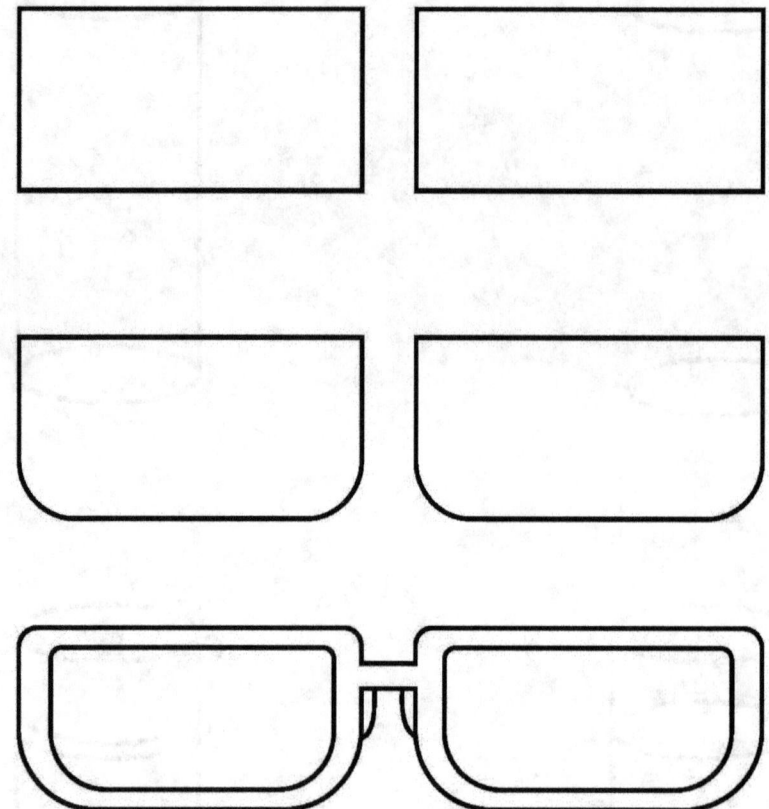

9. MUSIC PLAYER

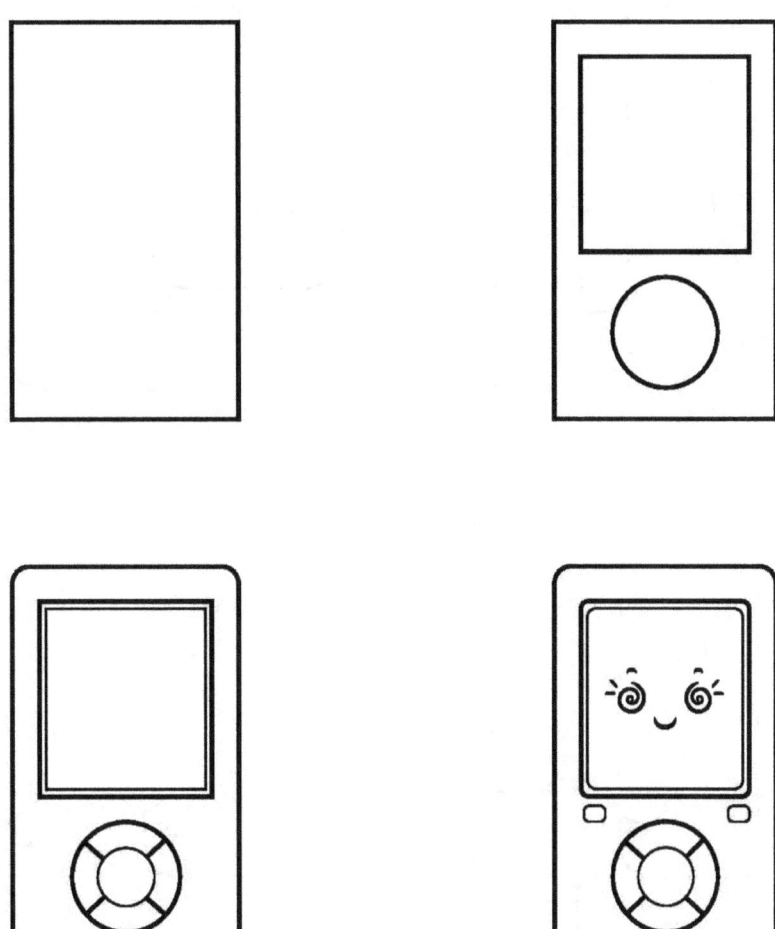

## 10. SOCKS

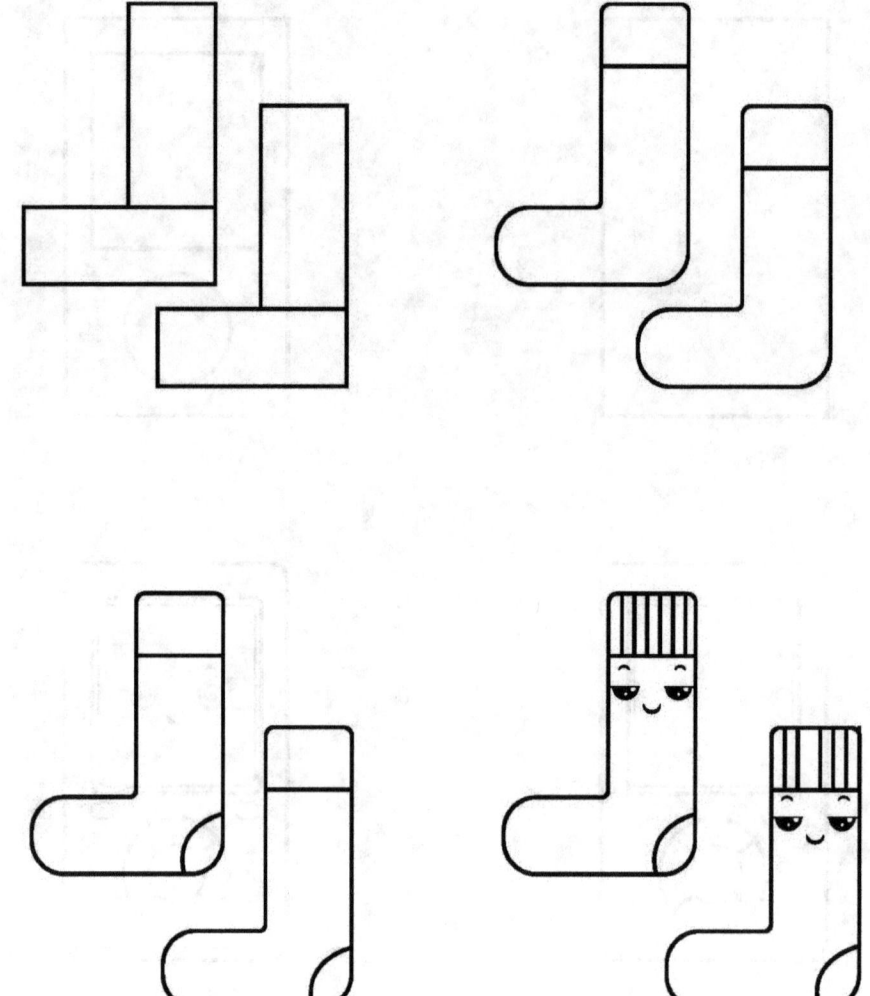

# KAWAII OBJECTS
## GIRL'S THINGS

Kawaii objects are easy to draw!
Since the rule in drawing cute is to simplify all the details, we will be using the most basic shapes then adjust some details to make it easier!

1. PURSE

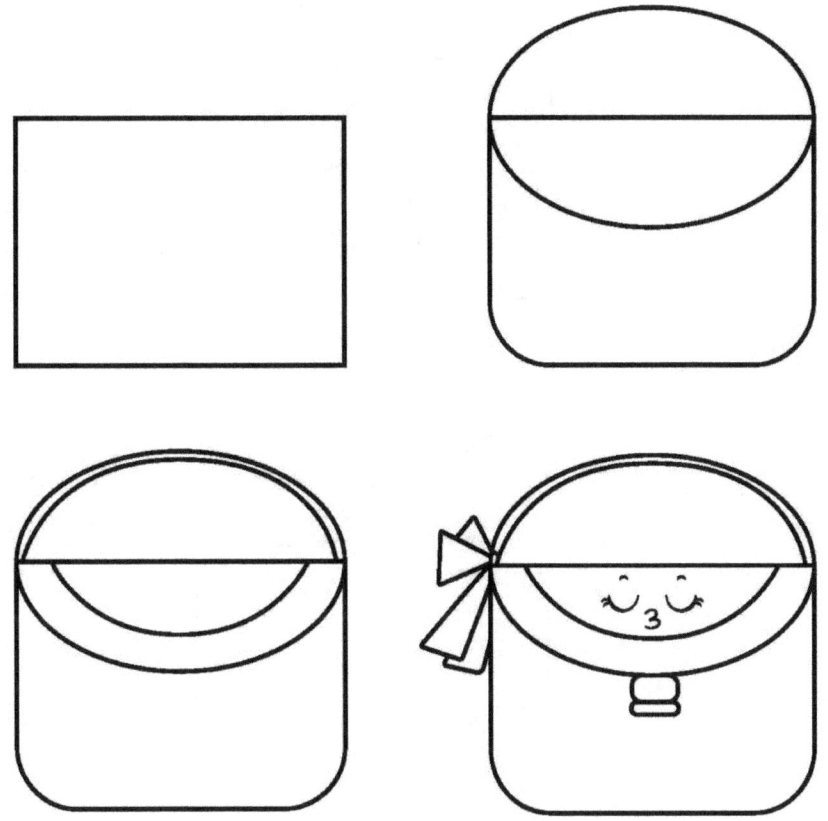

2. MAKEUP ITEMS

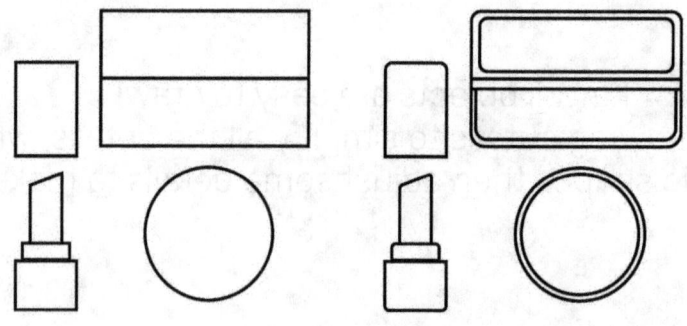

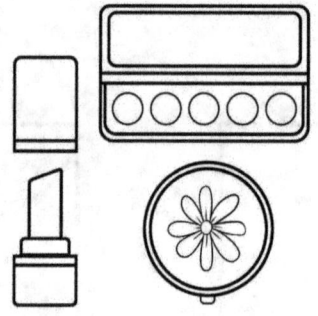

3. HAIR DRYER

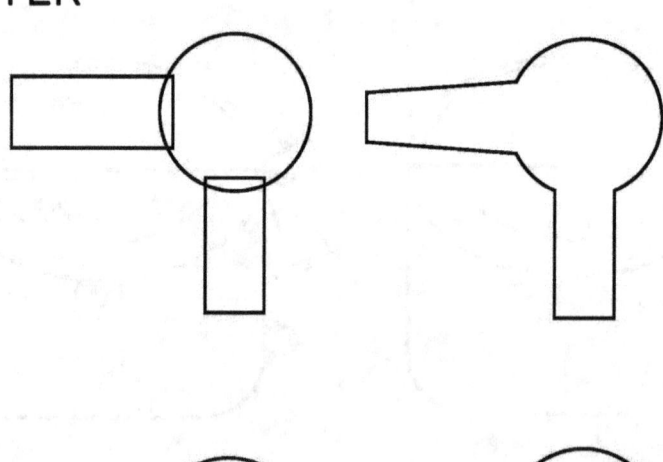

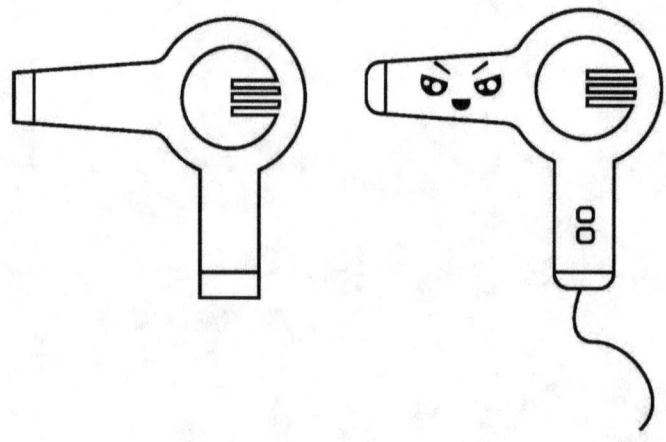

4. MOBILE PHONE

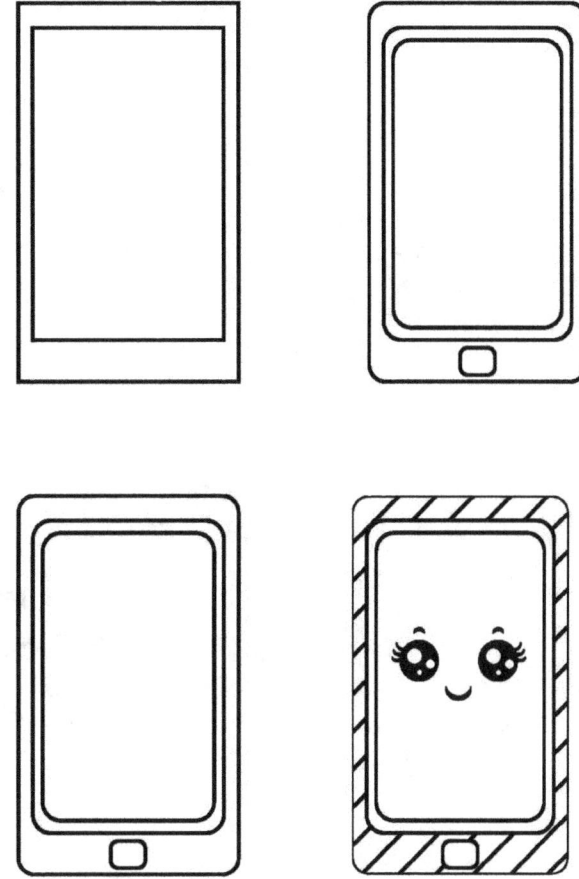

5. PERFUME

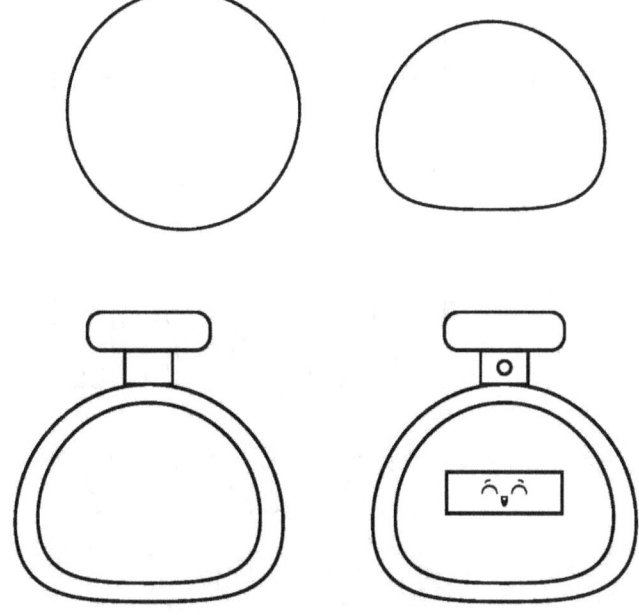

6. HAIR CLIPS AND TIES

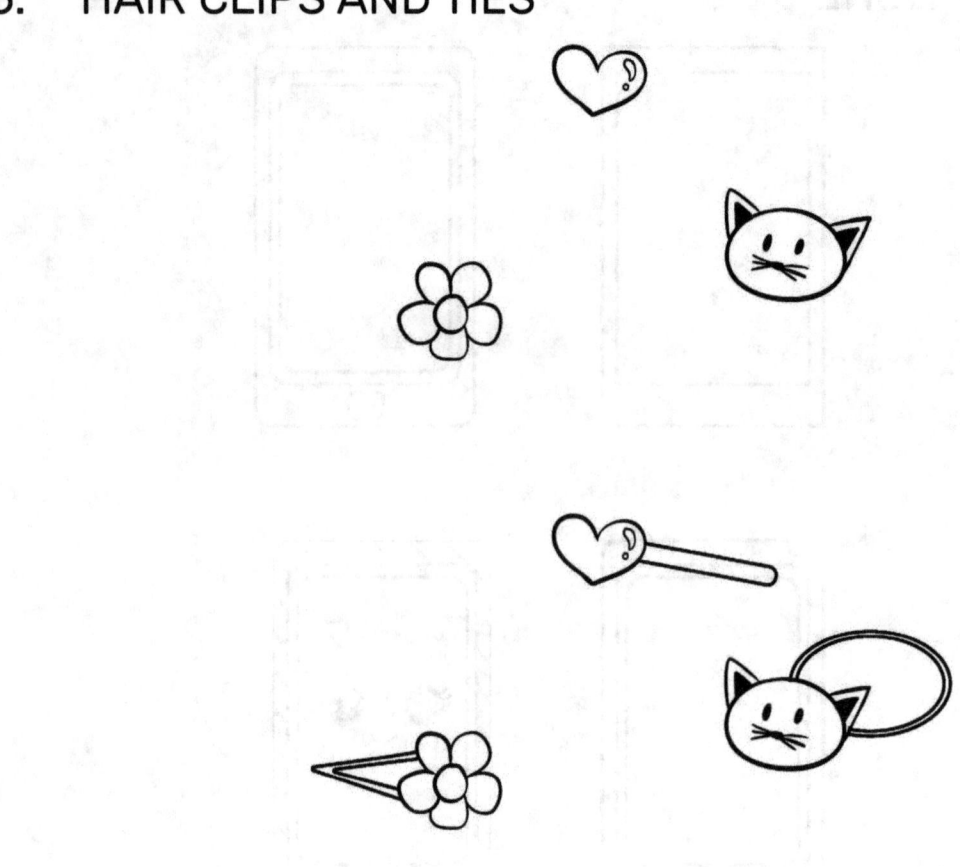

7. COMB

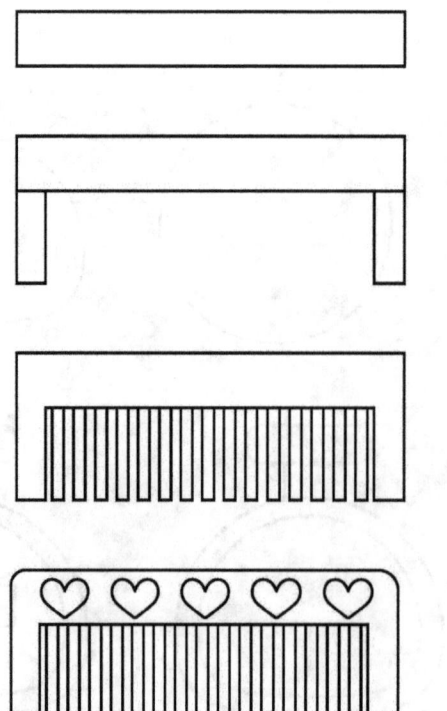

8. CAMERA

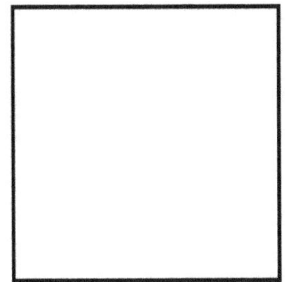
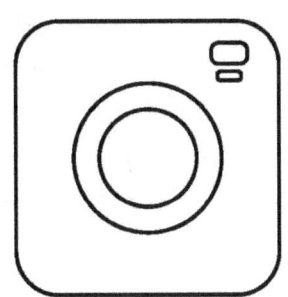
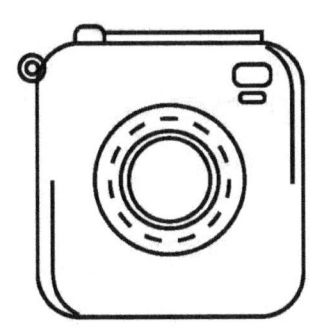
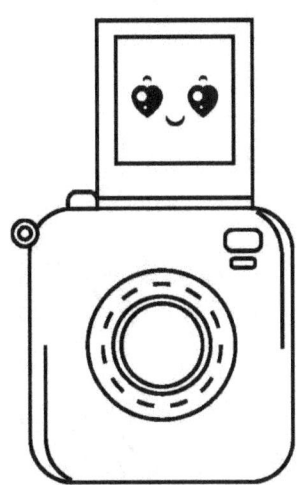

9. WALLET

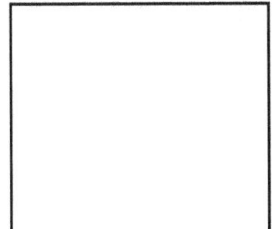

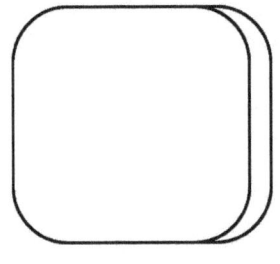
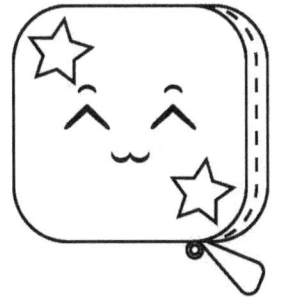

## 10. SUNGLASSES

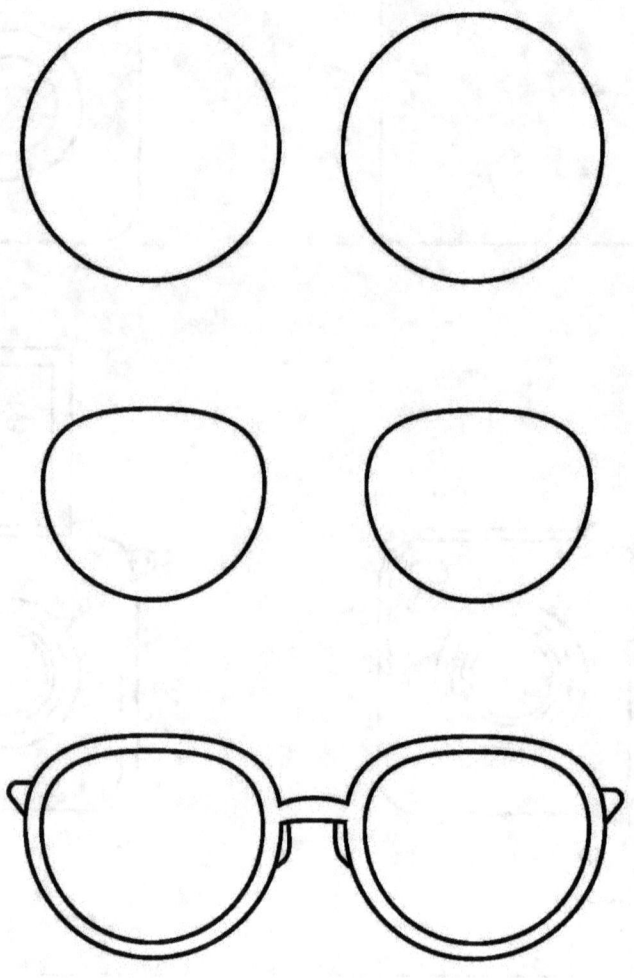

# KAWAII OBJECTS
## SCHOOL THINGS

1. NOTEBOOKS

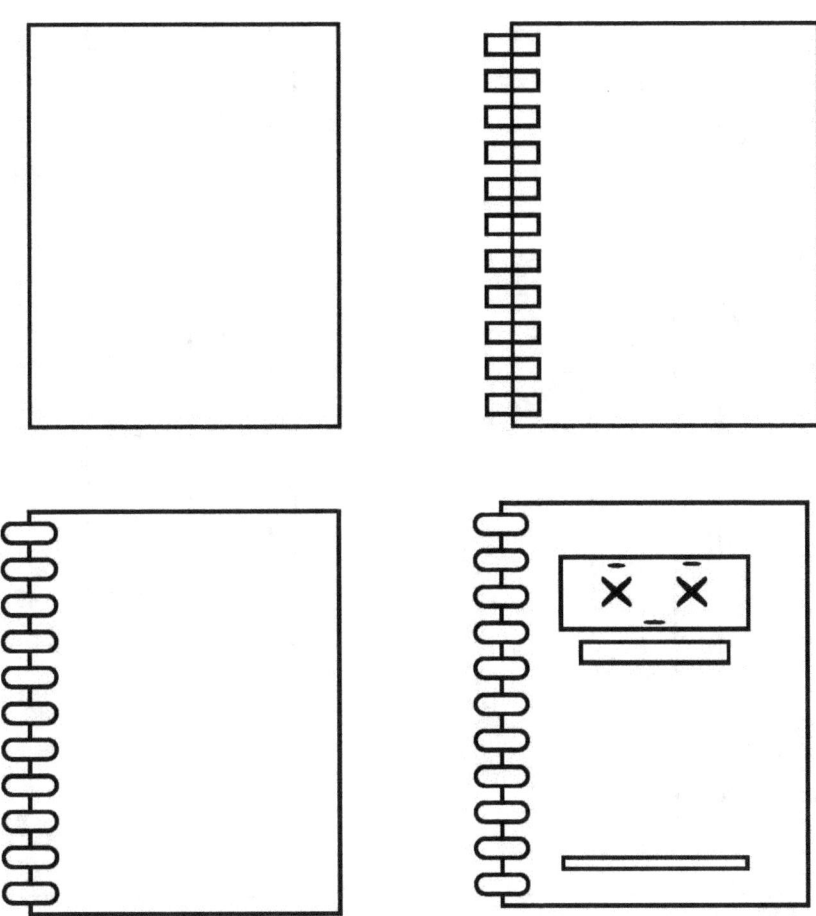

85

2. PENS

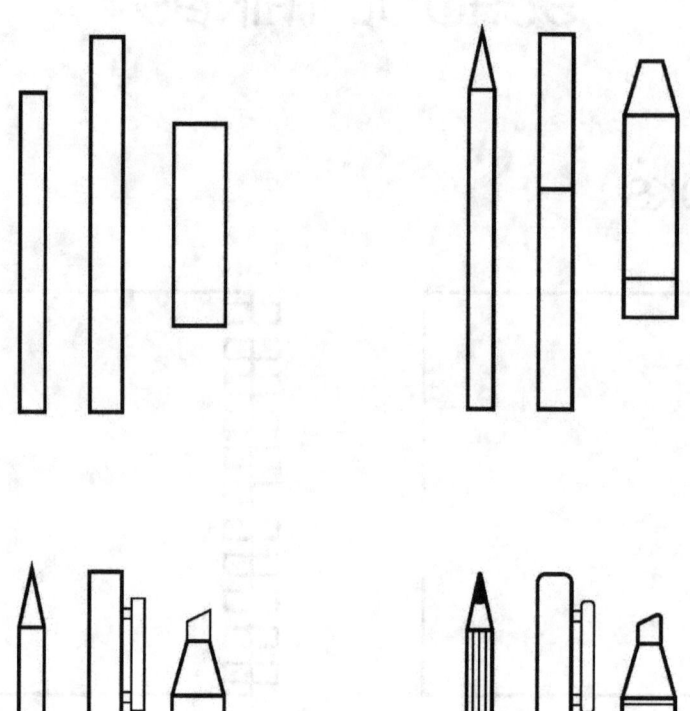

3. PENCIL CASE

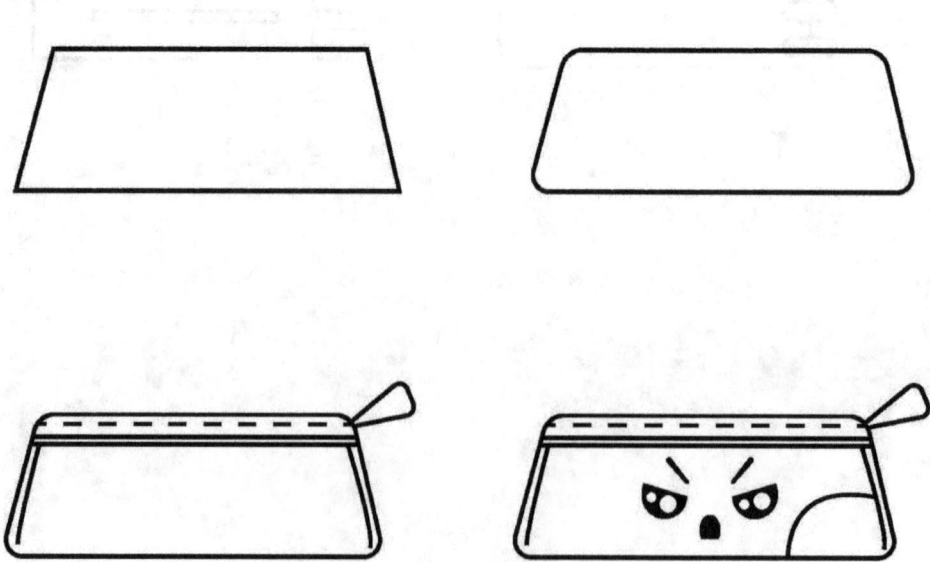

4. SCHOOL BAG

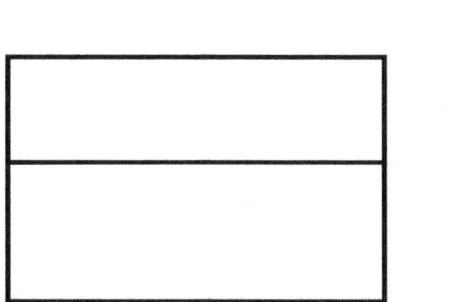
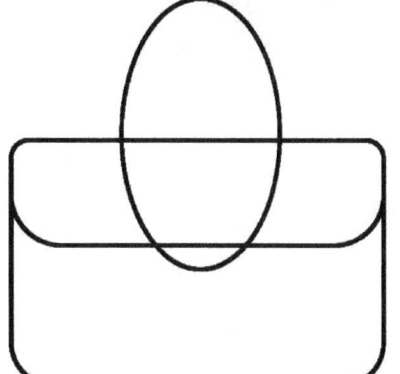
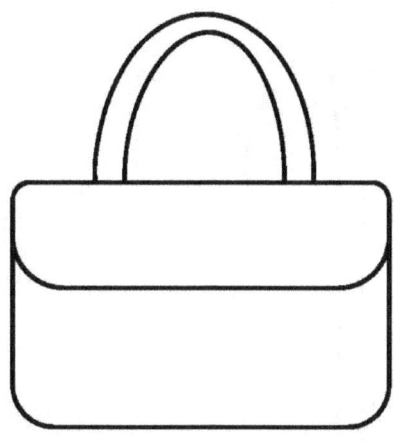
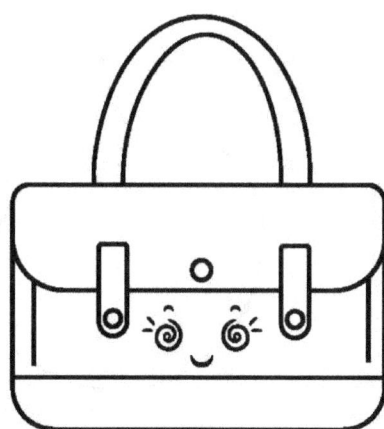

5. CALCULATOR

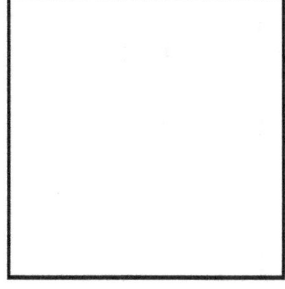

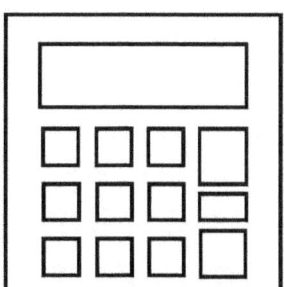
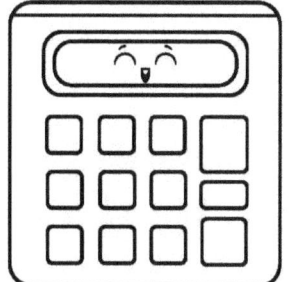

## 6. ART SUPPLIES

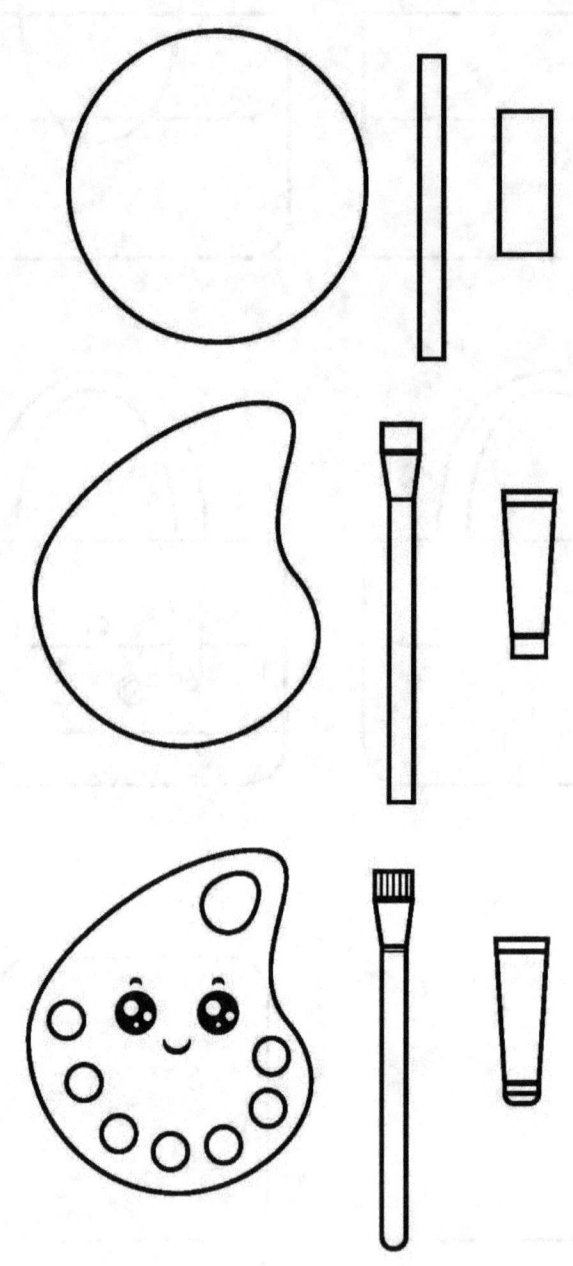

7. GLUE

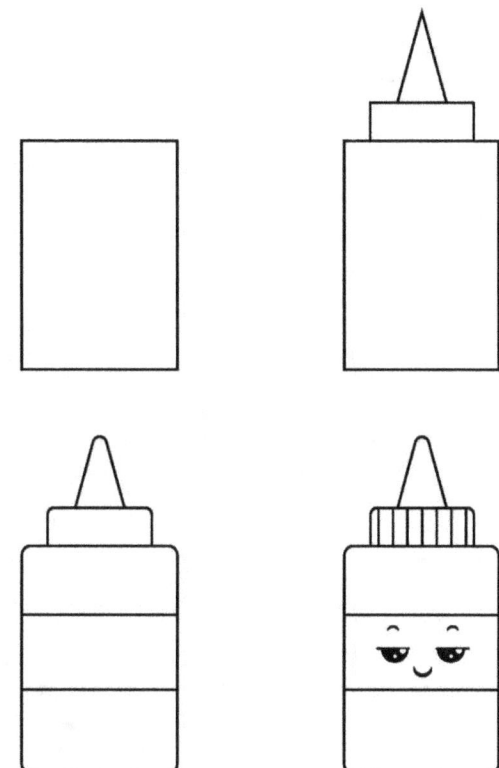

8. LUNCHBOX

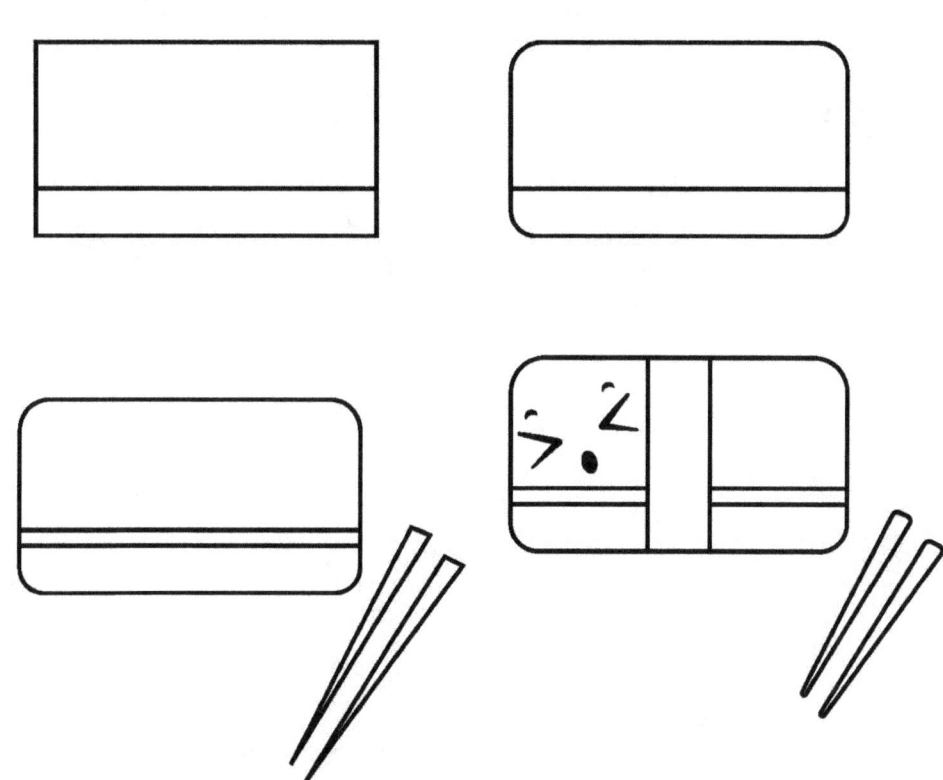

9. JOURNAL

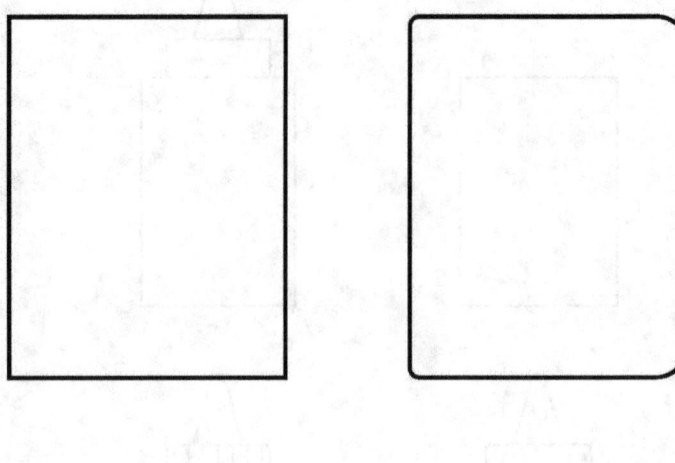

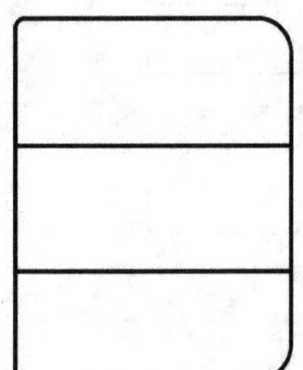
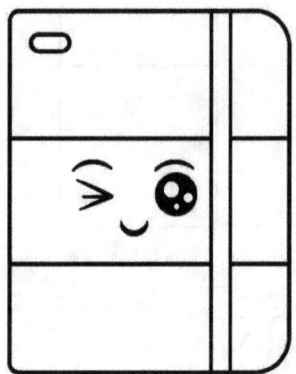

10. SCISSORS

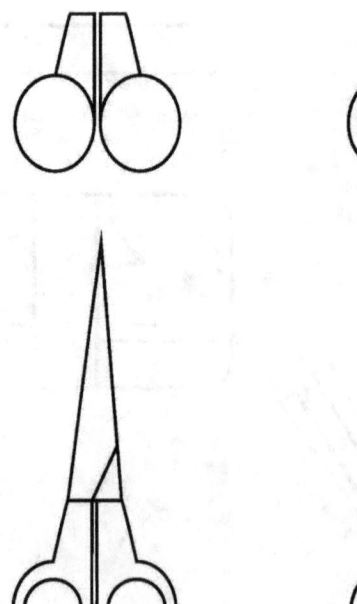
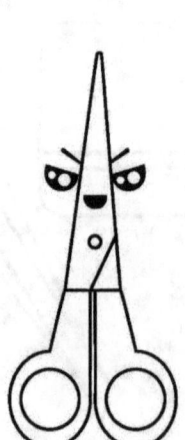

# KAWAII OBJECTS
## FURNITURE

1. BED

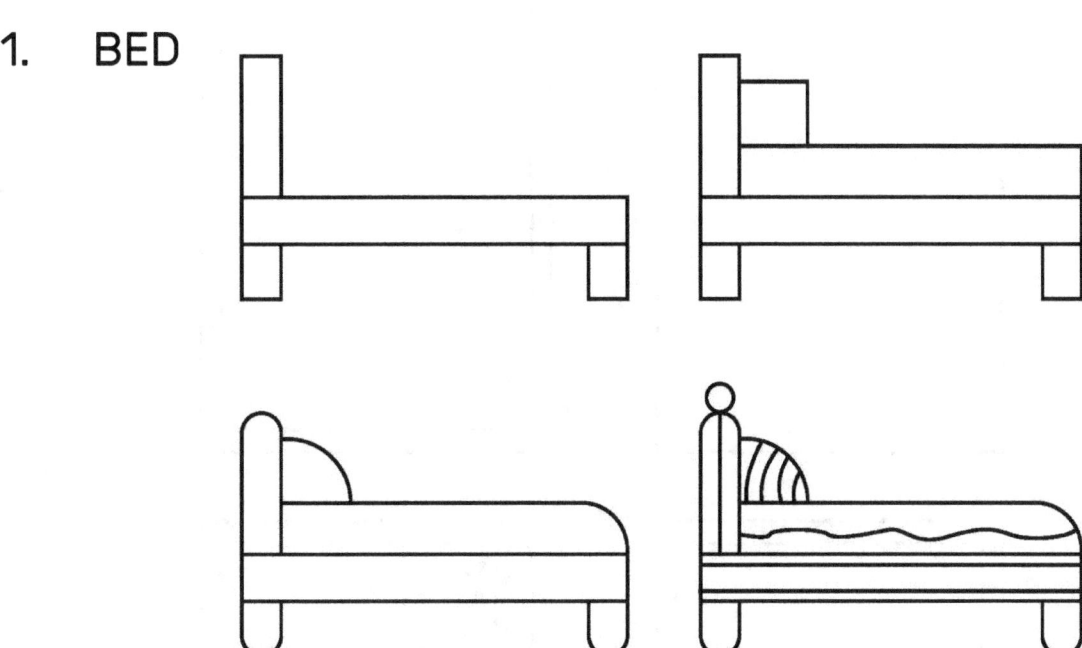

2. VANITY

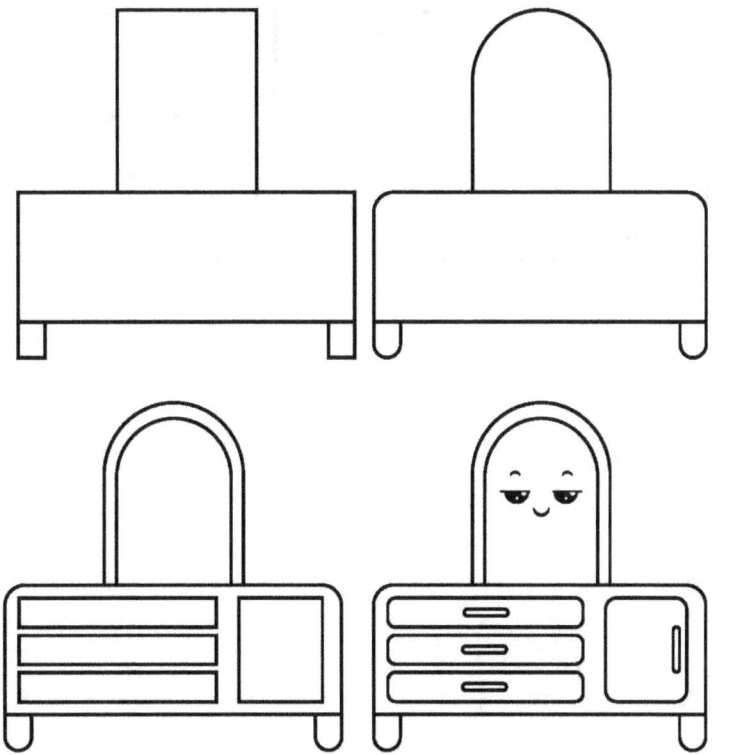

3. BOOKSHELF

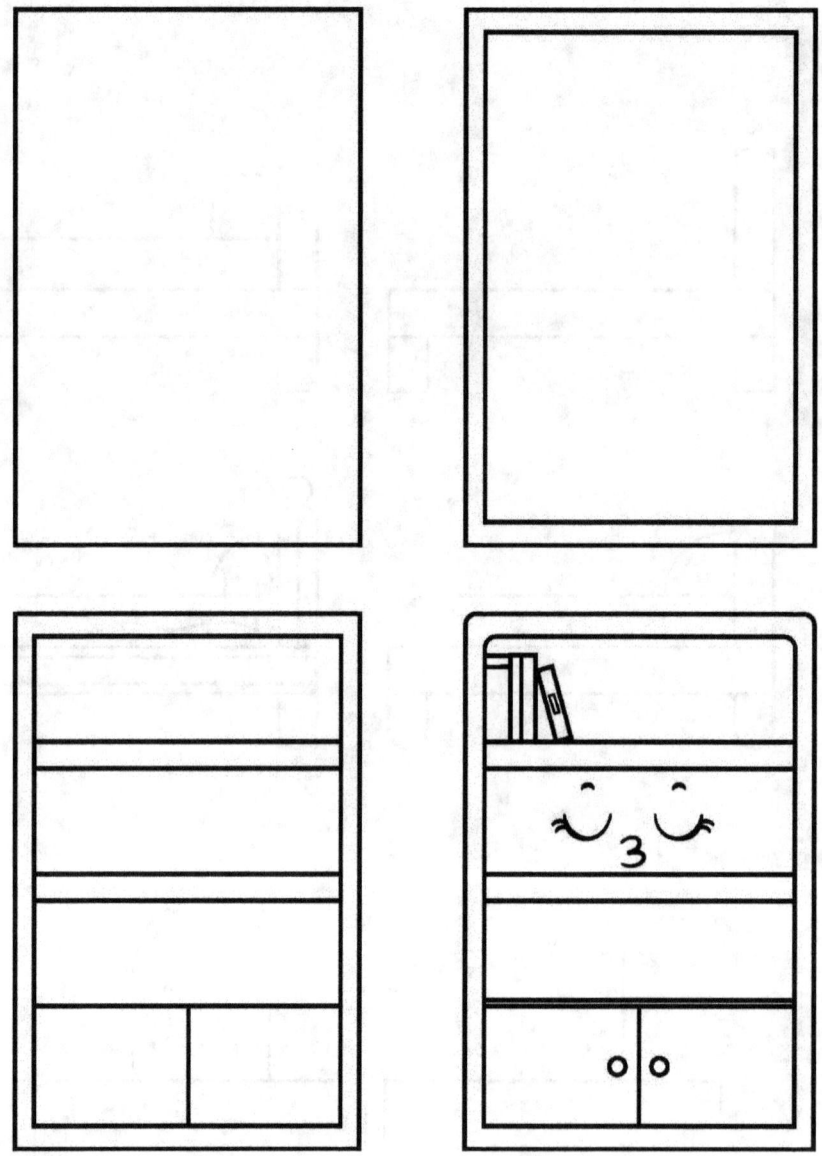

## 4. WARDROBE

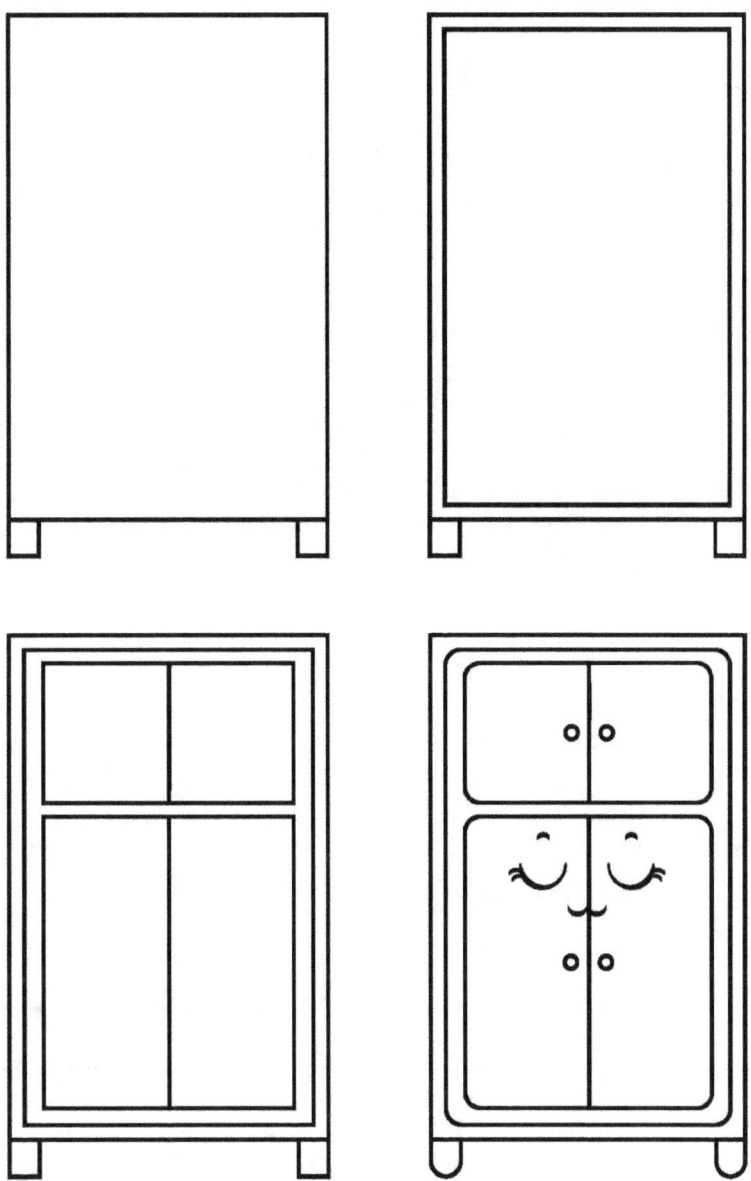

5. STUDY DESK

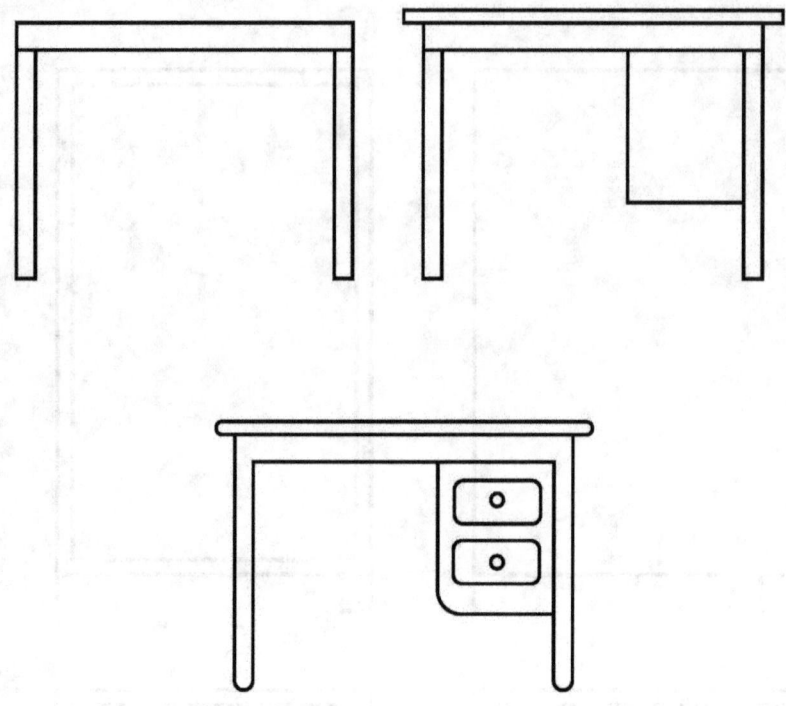

6. COUCH

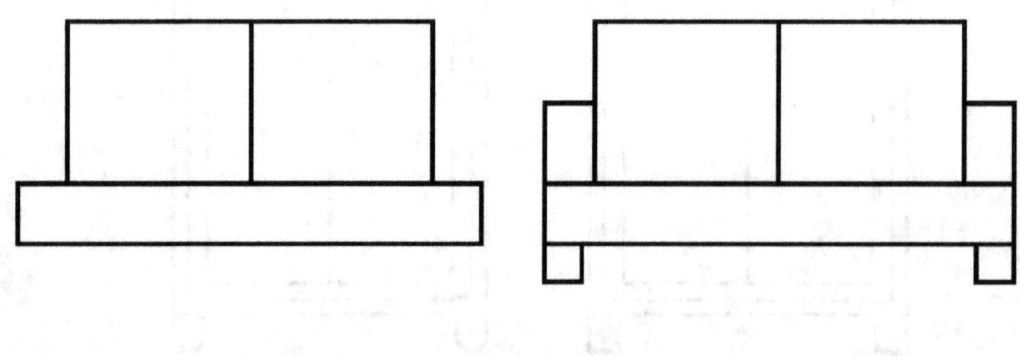

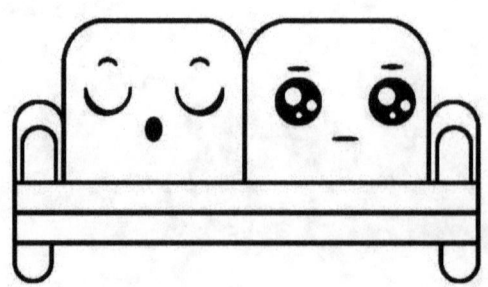

7. MIRROR

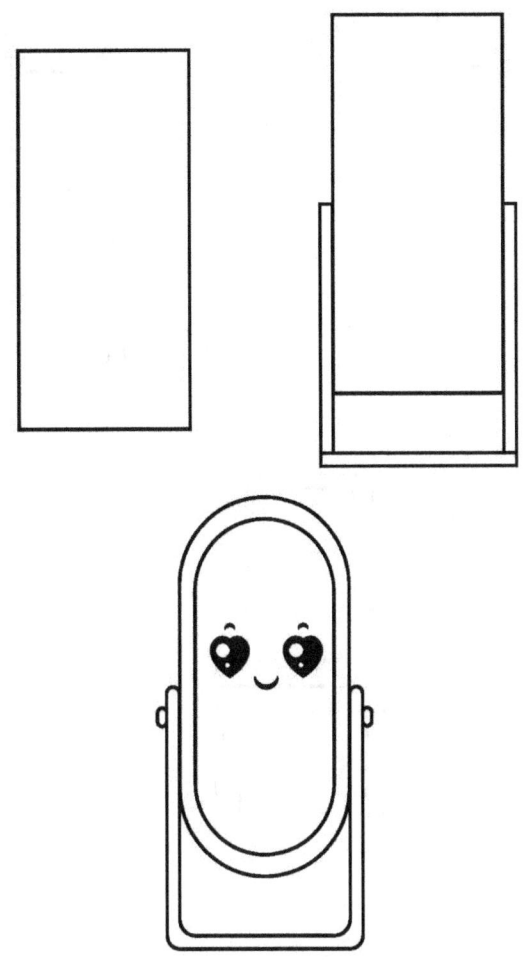

8. TABLE

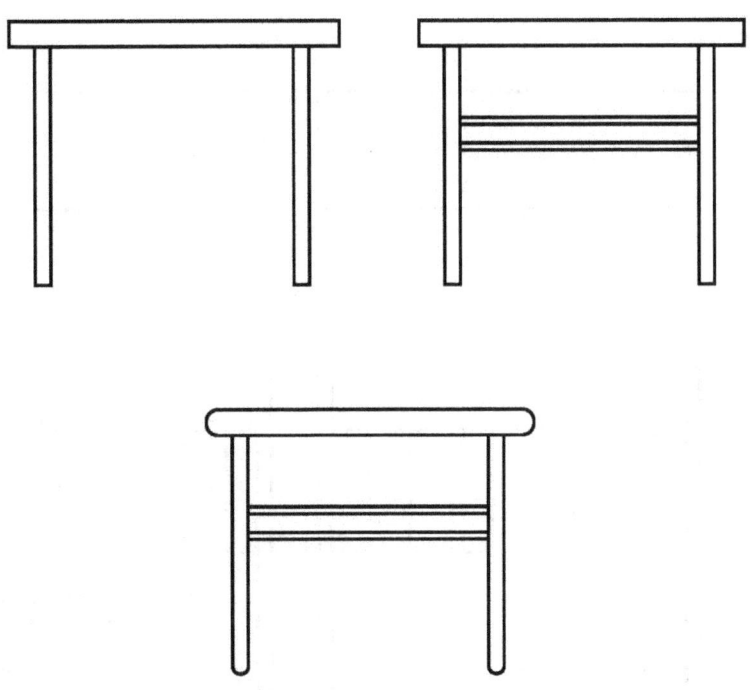

9. CHAIR

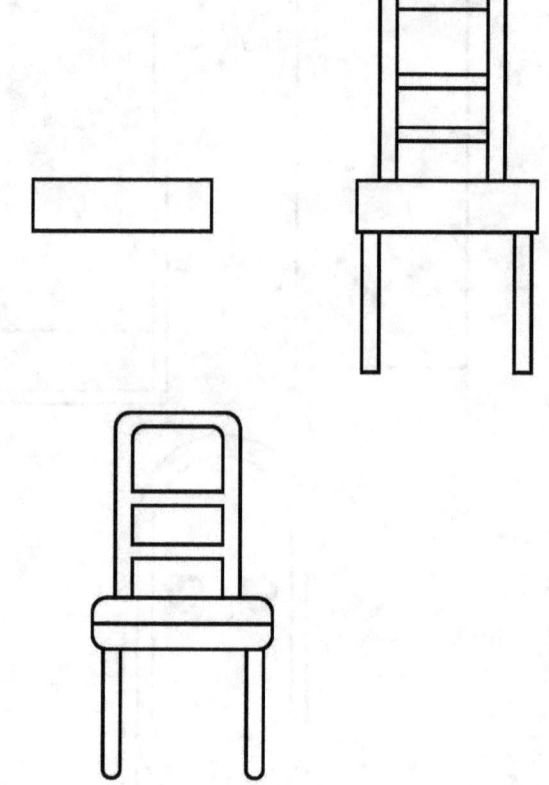

10. BABIES' CRIB

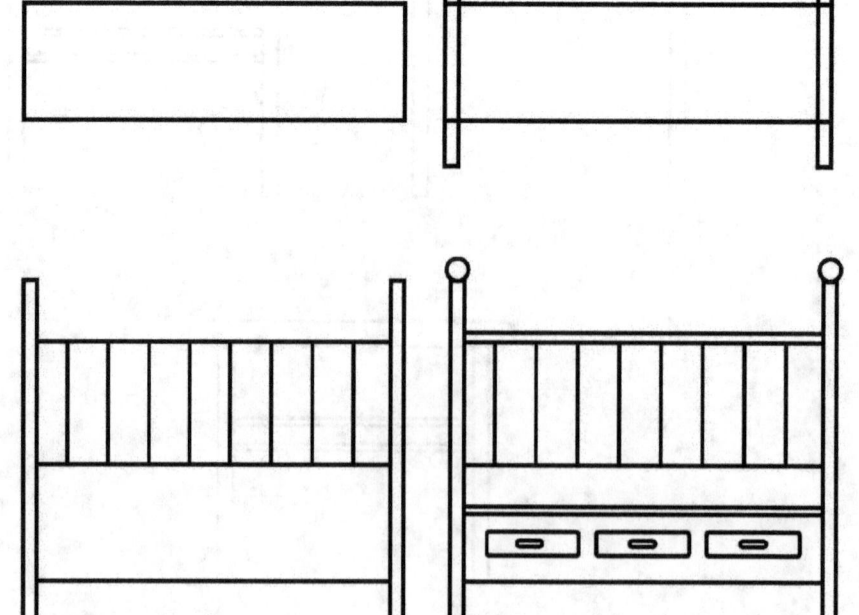

# KAWAII OBJECTS
## KITCHEN THINGS

1. CASSEROLE POT

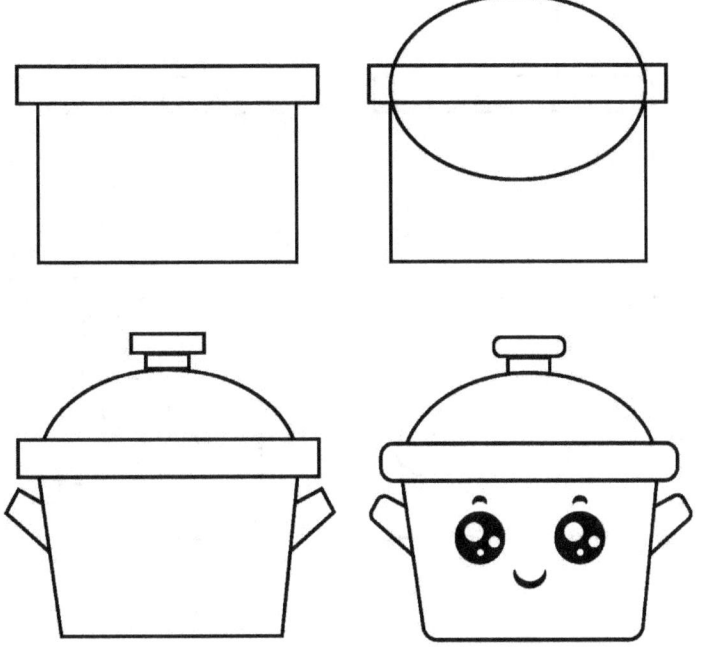

2. KETTLE

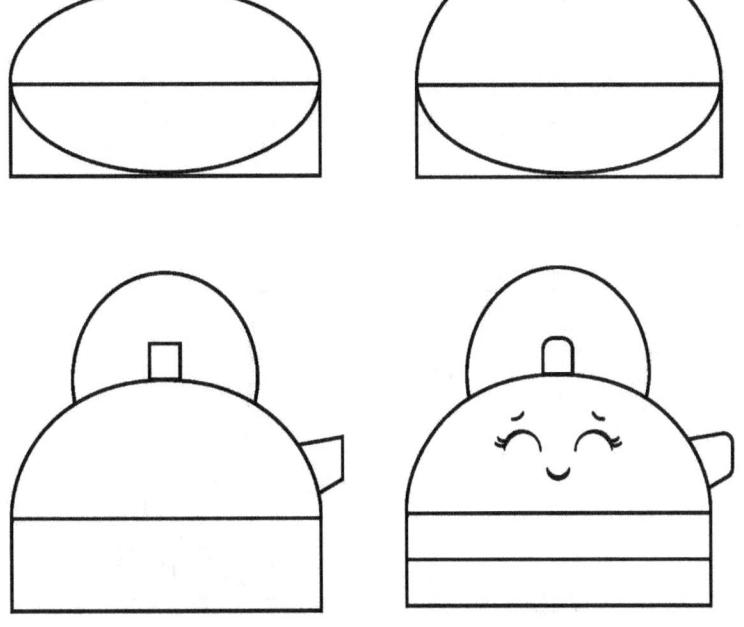

3. MIXER

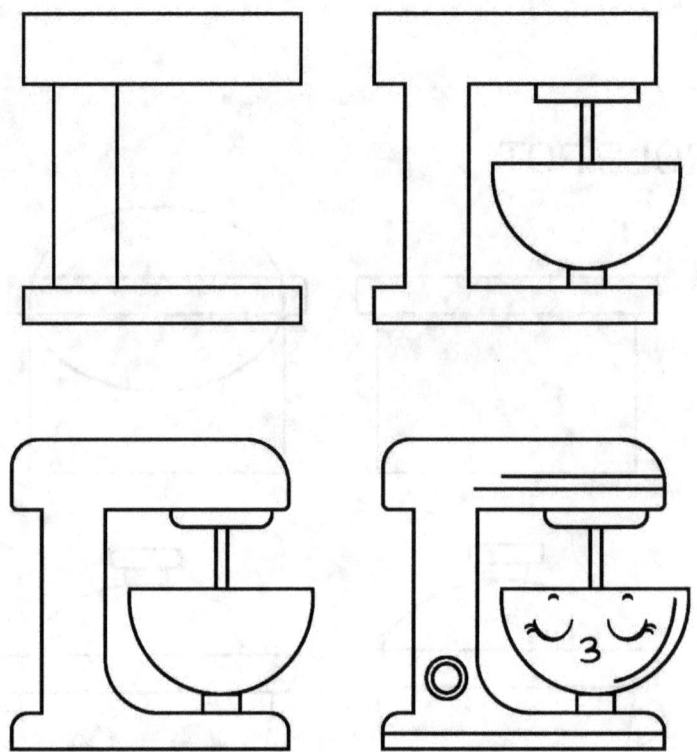

4. BLENDER

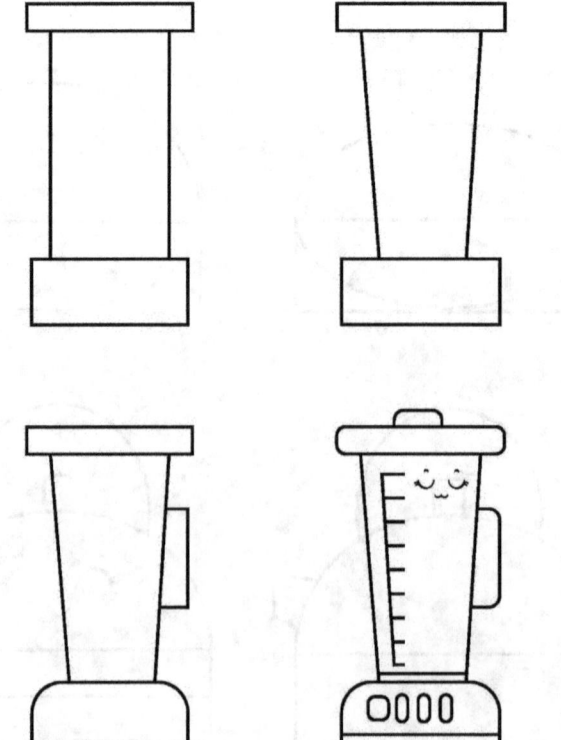

## 5. FRYING PAN

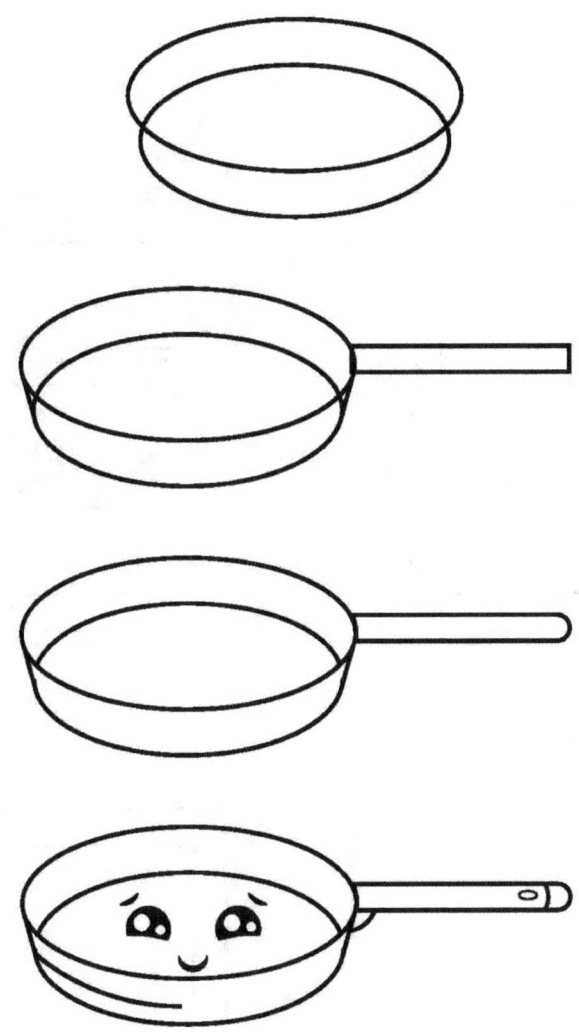

6. COFFEE POT

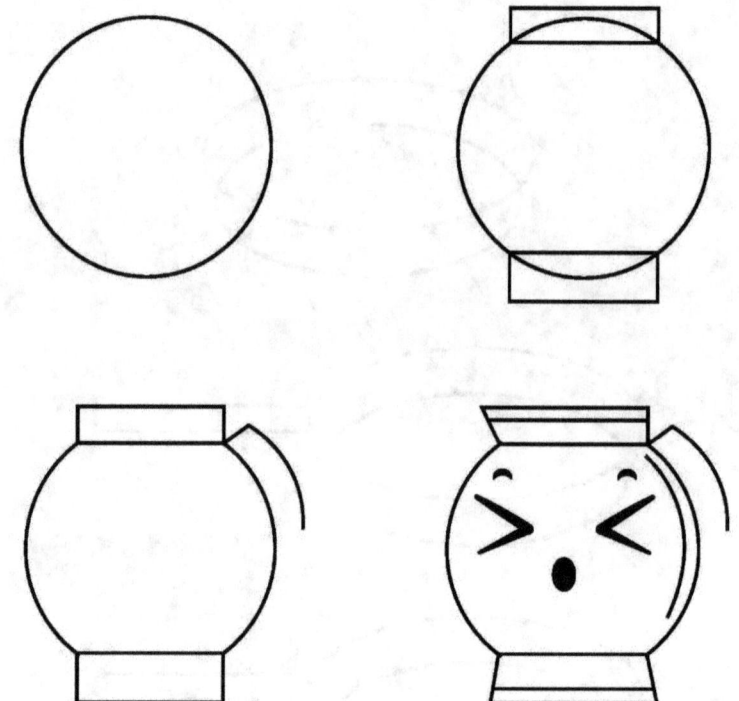

7. MICROWAVE

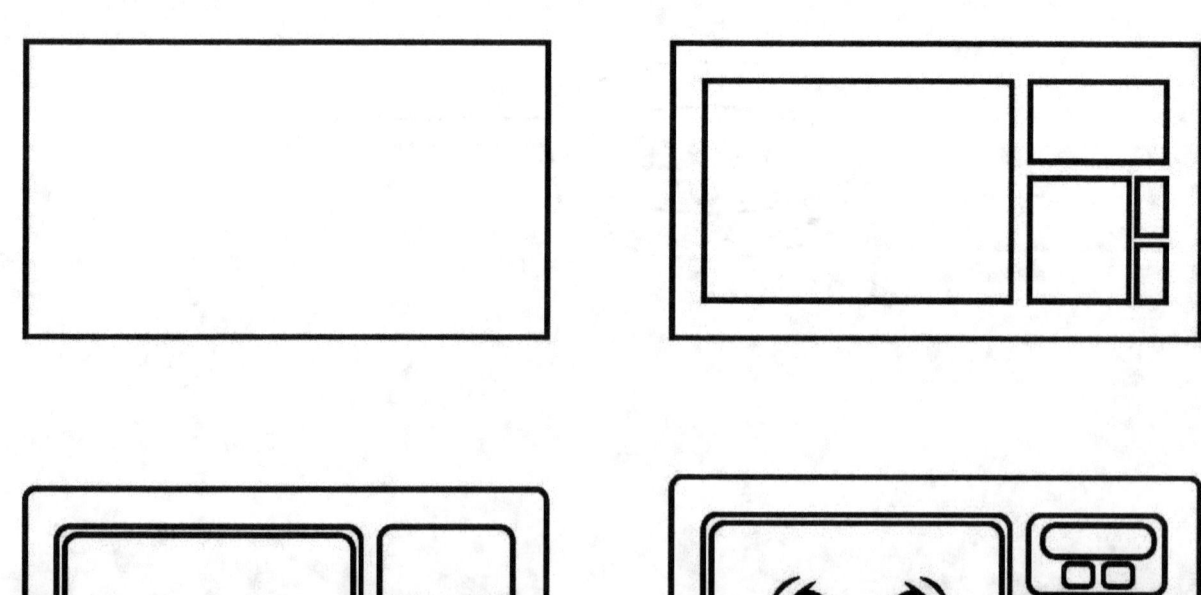

8. BREAD TOASTER

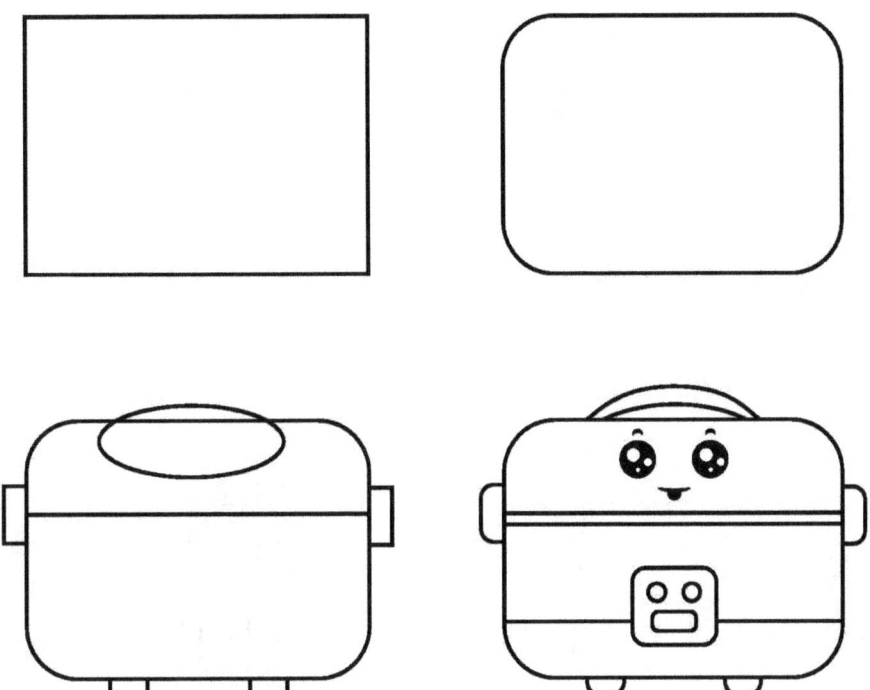

9. RICE COOKER

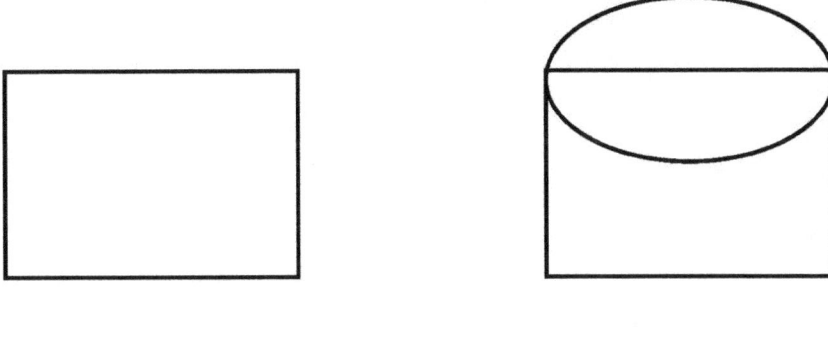

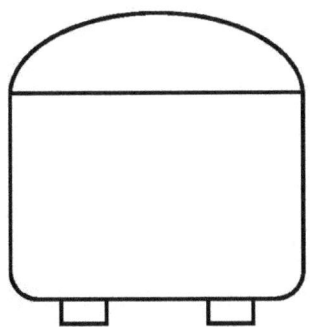
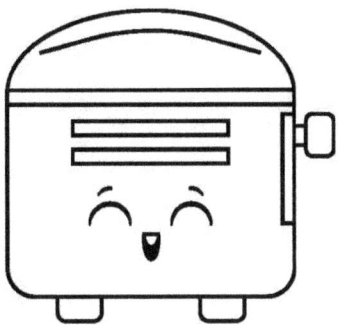

## 10. SHAKERS

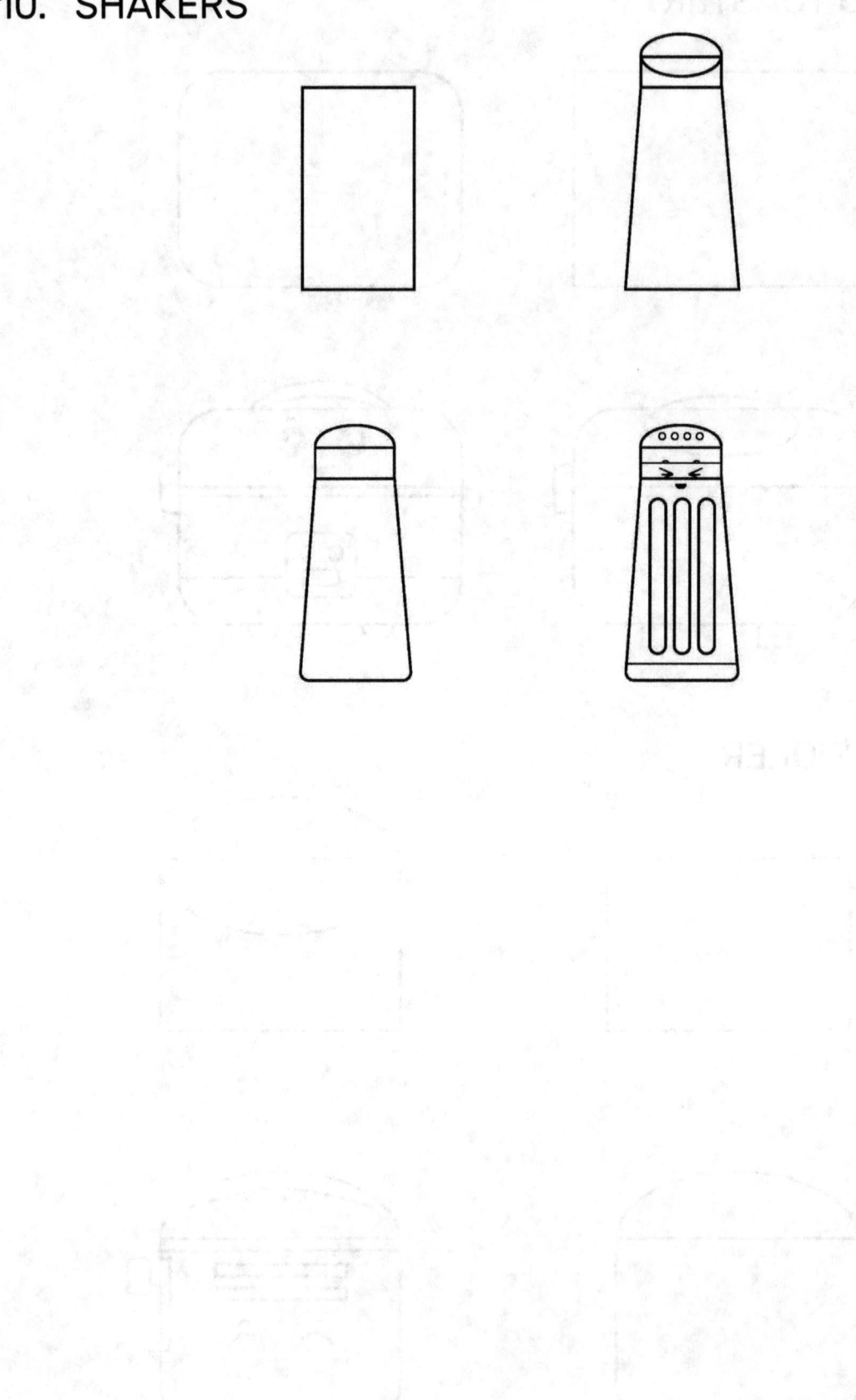

# KAWAII OBJECTS
## BATHROOM THINGS

1. **RUBBER DUCK**

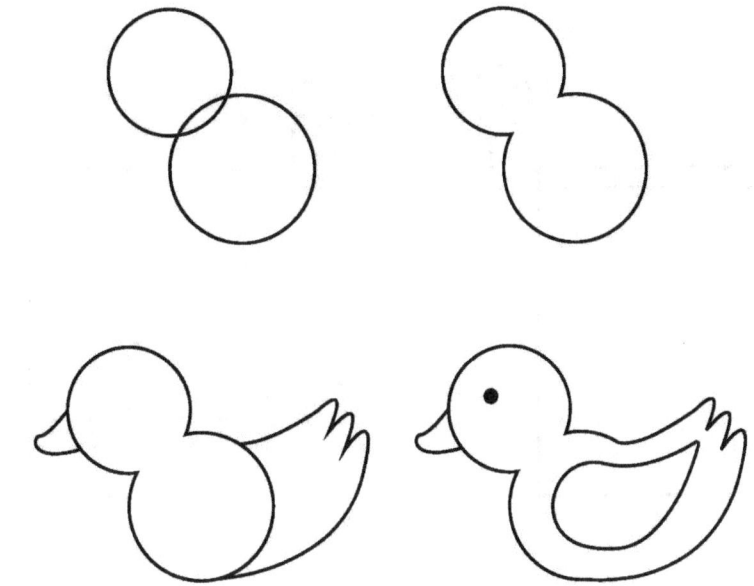

2. **SHAMPOO**

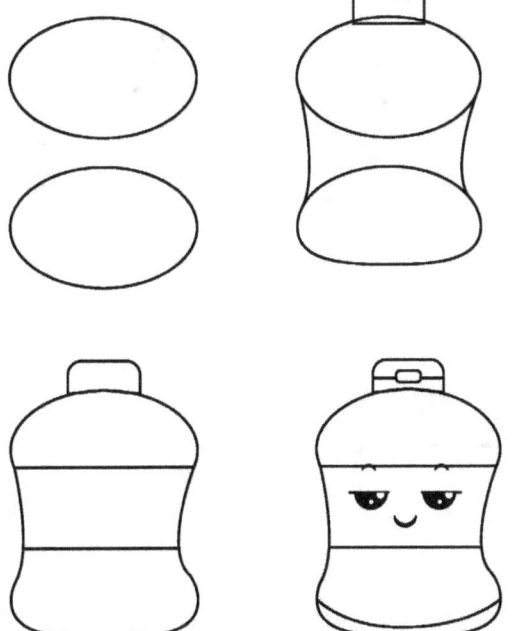

3. TOWEL RACK

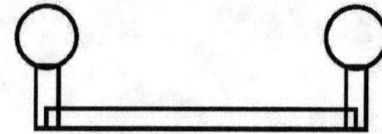 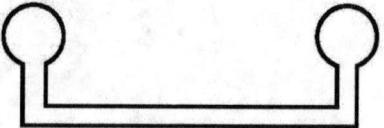

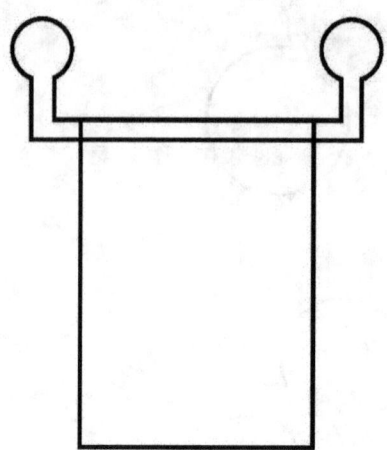 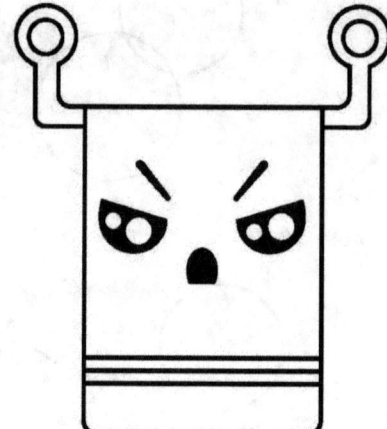

4. BATHTUB

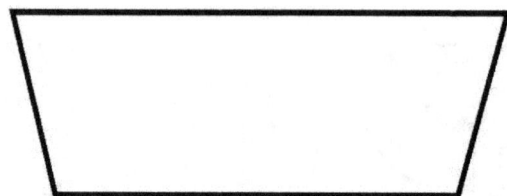 

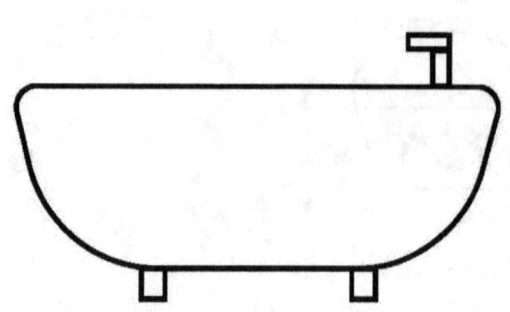 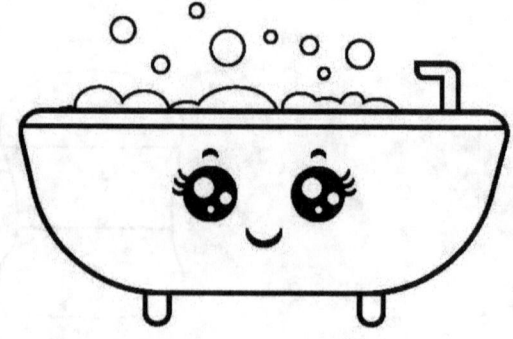

5. TOOTHBRUSH

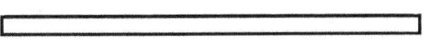

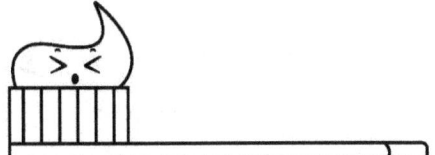

6. TOOTHPASTE

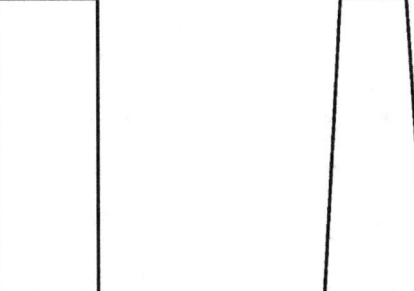

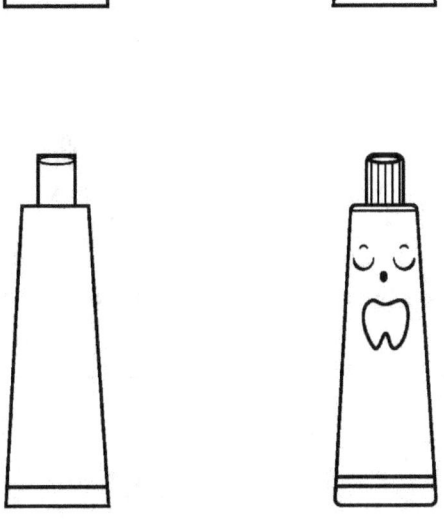

7. **TOILET PAPER**

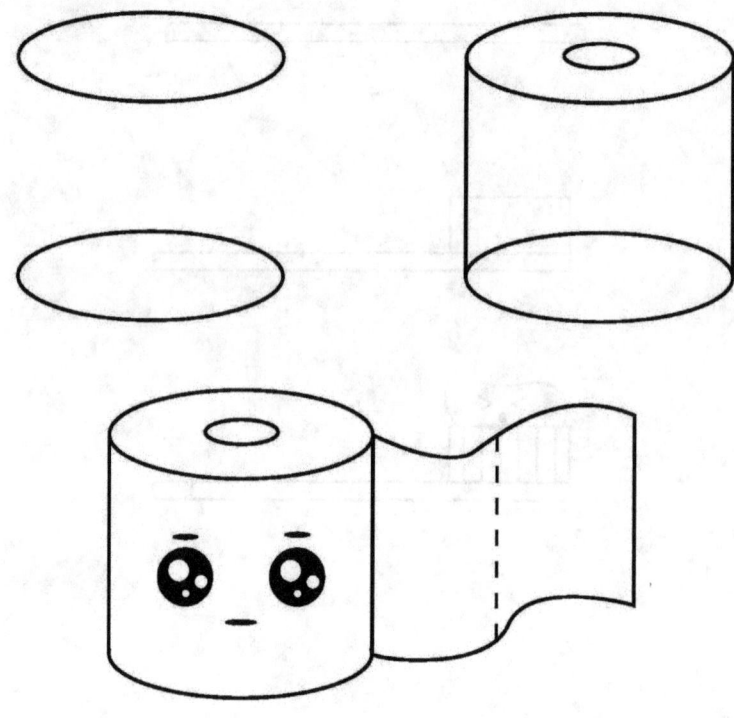

8. **BODY WASH**

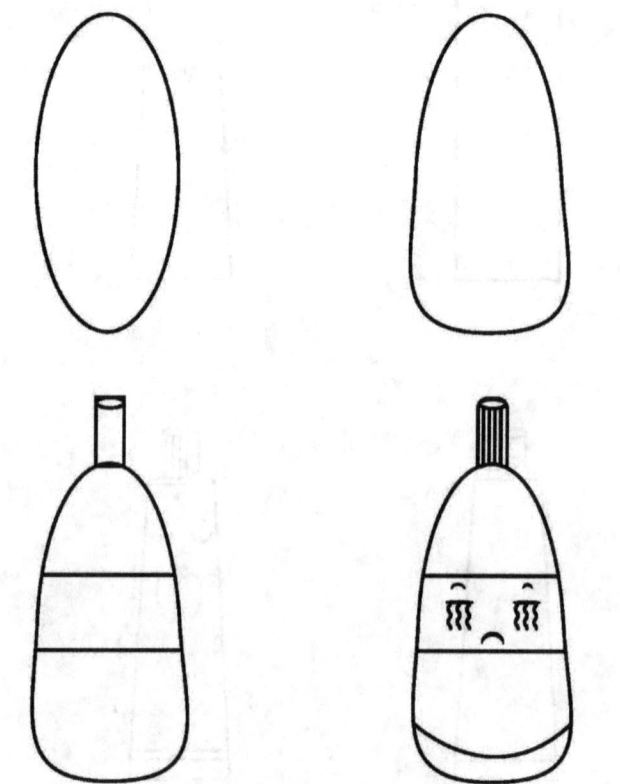

9. SHOWER BRUSH

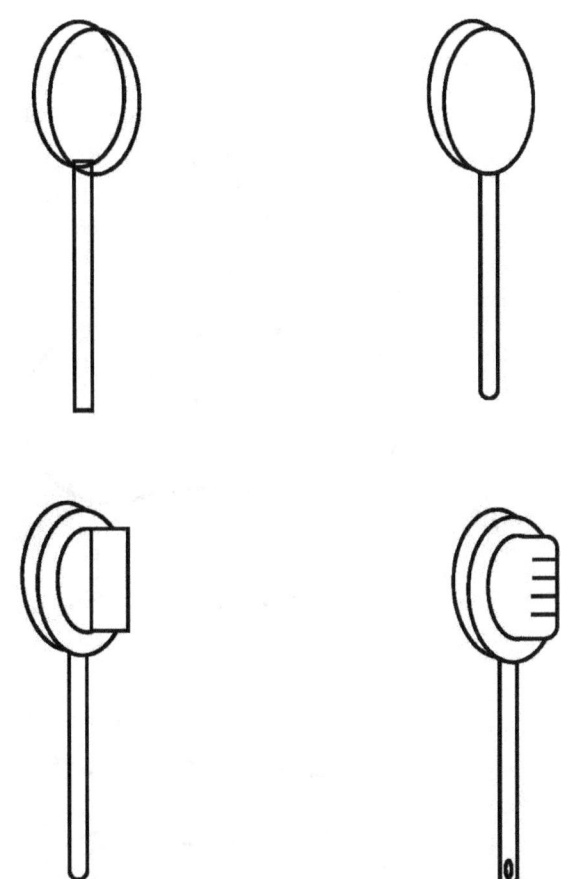

10. BAR OF SOAP

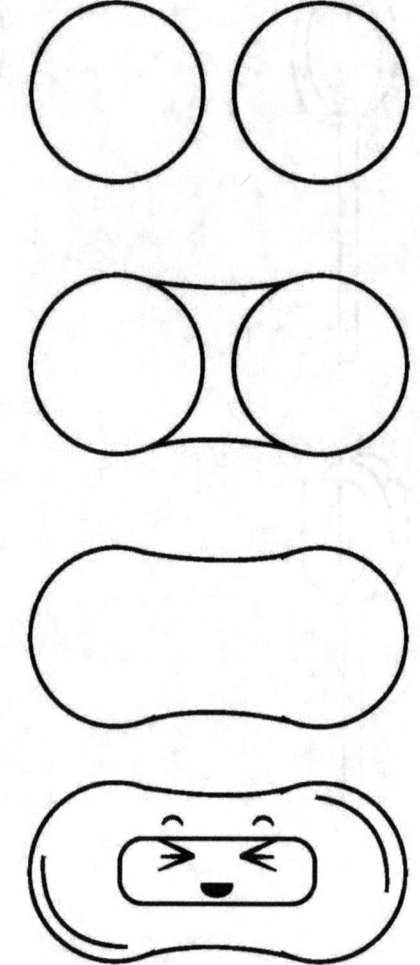

# KAWAII OBJECTS
## CLEANING THINGS

1. WASHING MACHINE

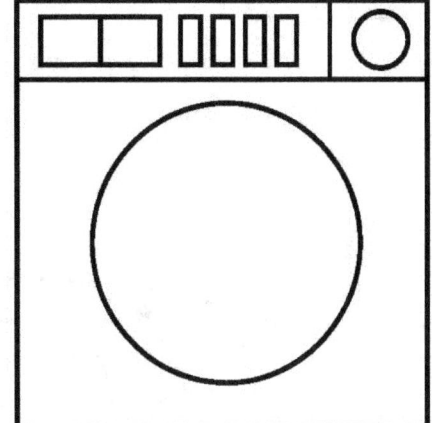
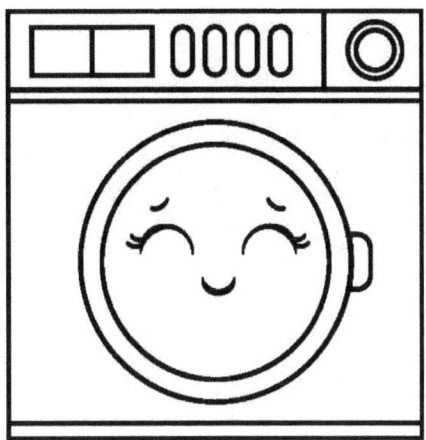

2. VACUUM CLEANER

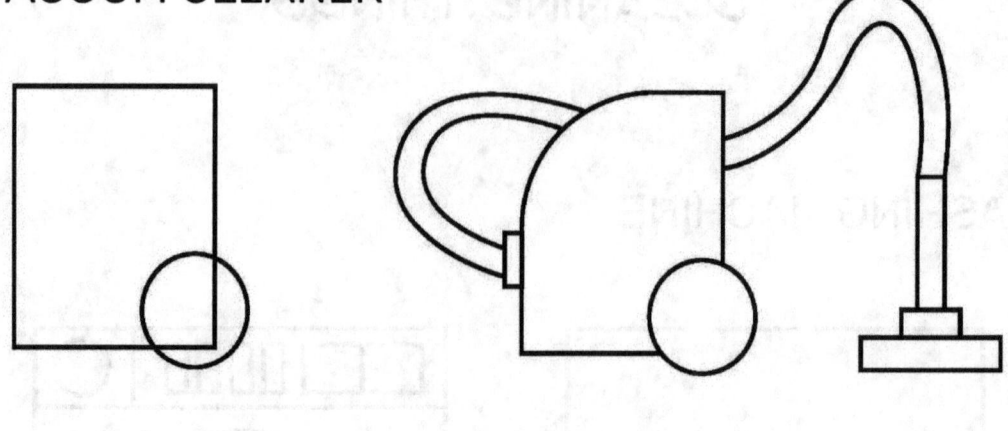

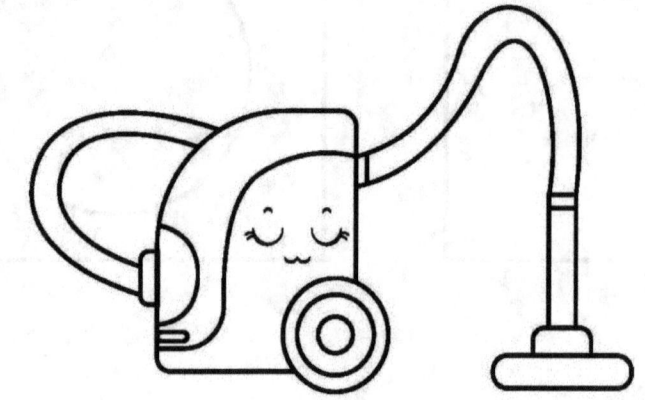

3. BROOM

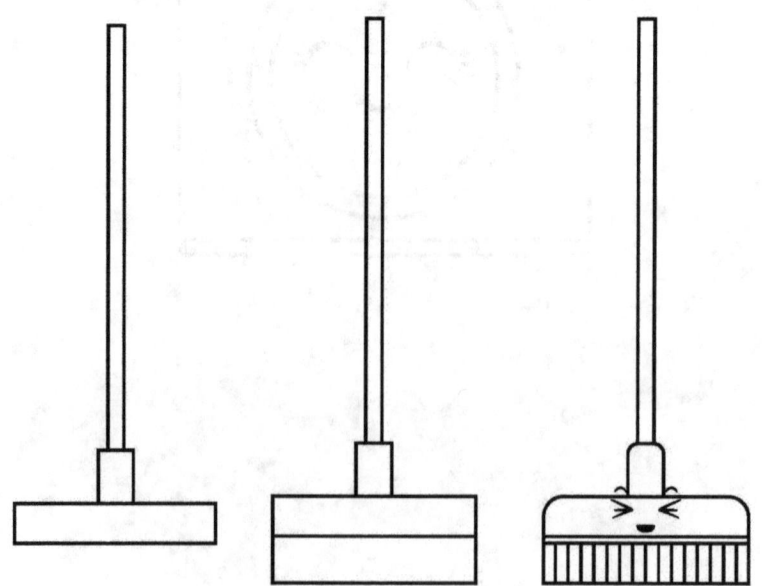

4. IRON

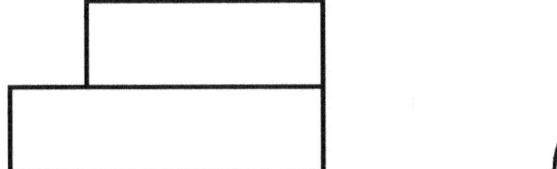

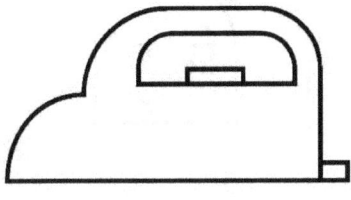
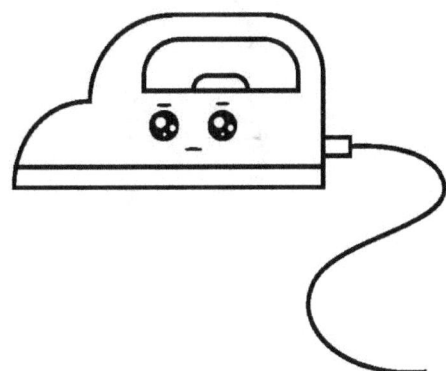

5. WATER SPRAYER

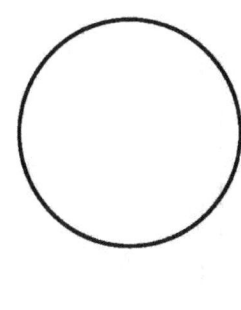
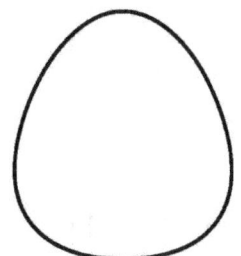

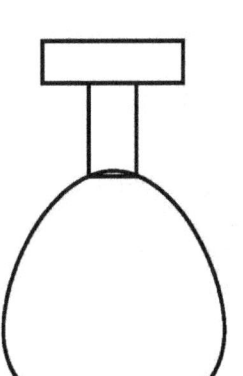
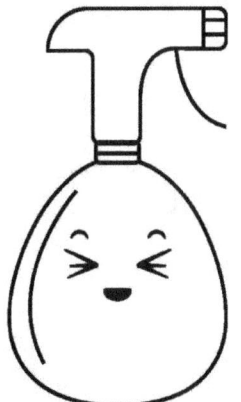

## 6. TOILET PLUNGER

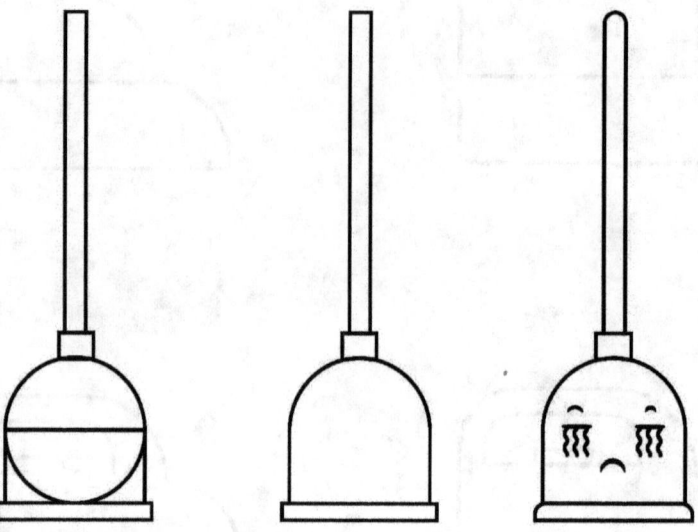

## 7. FLOOR WIPER

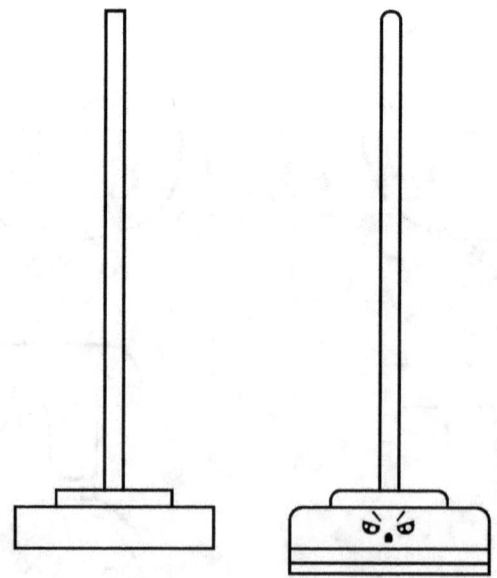

## 8. IRONING BOARD

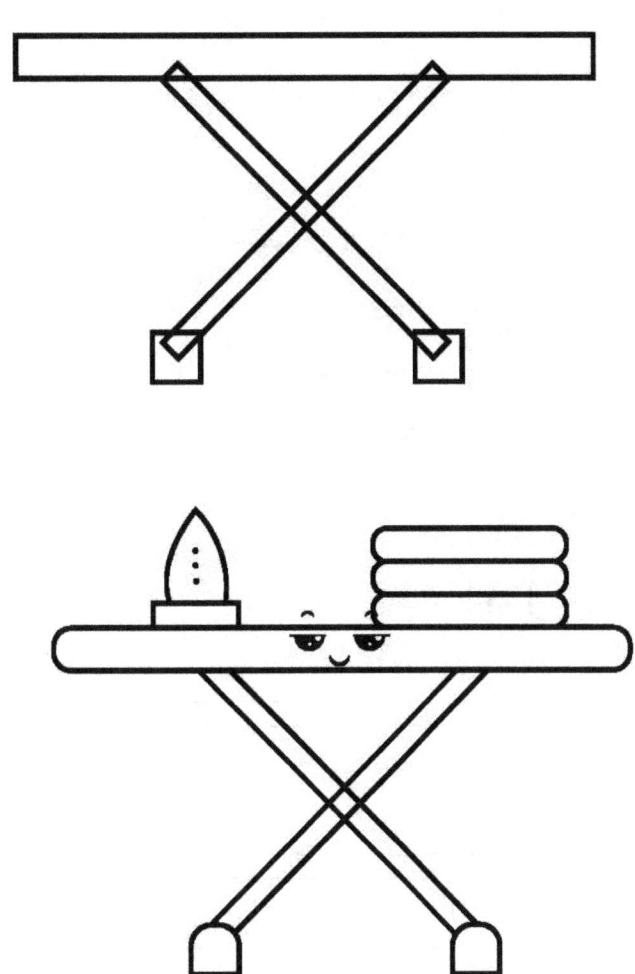

9. SPONGE

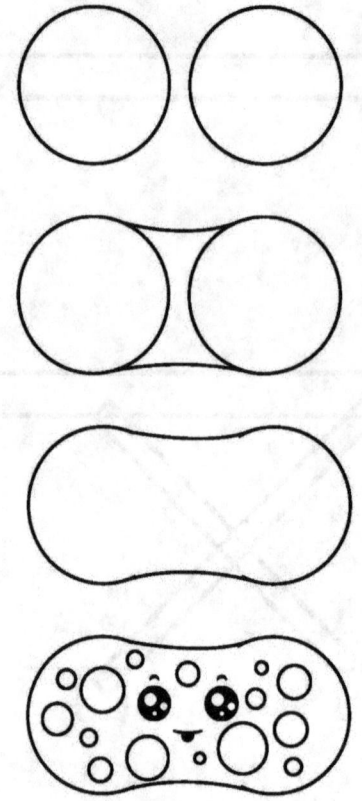

10. CLEANING BRUSH

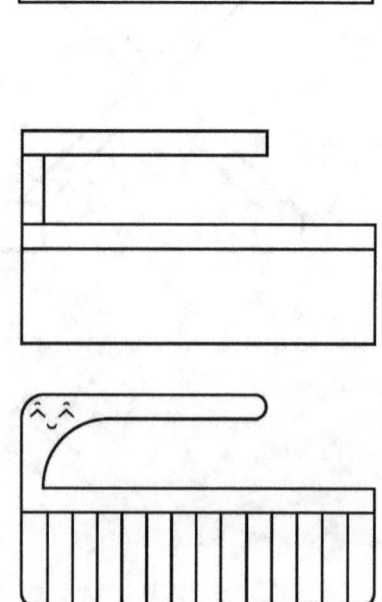

# KAWAII OBJECTS
## BEACH THINGS

1. BEACH BALL

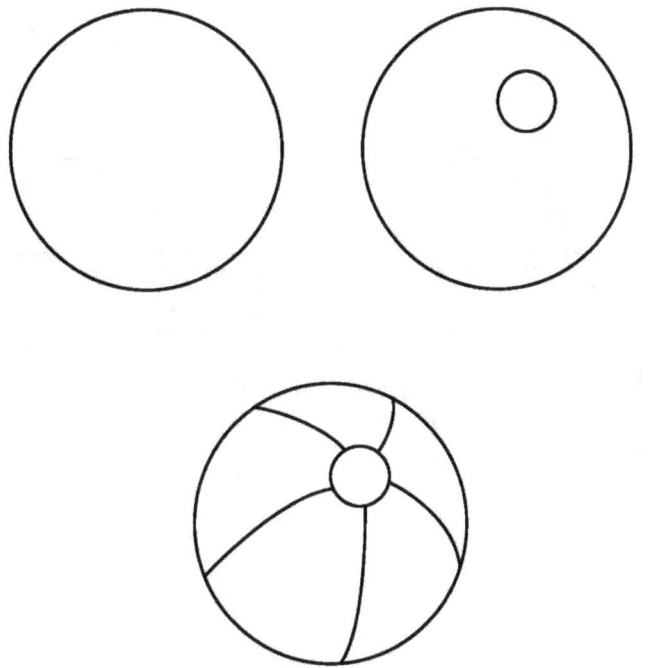

2. FLOATER

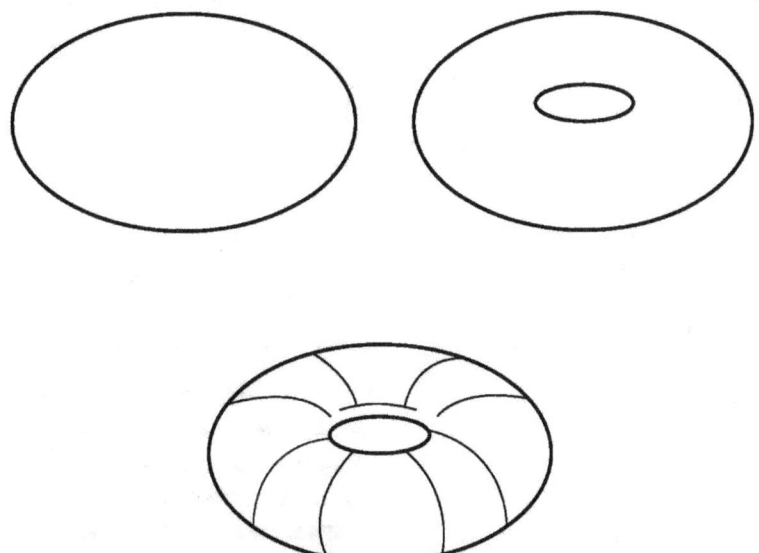

3. TOY PAIL

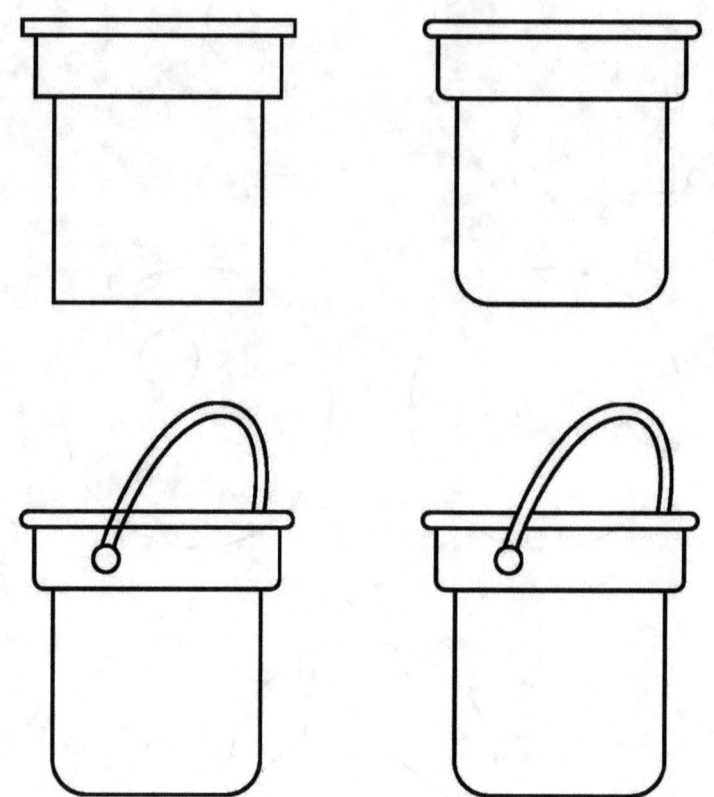

4. BEACH BAG

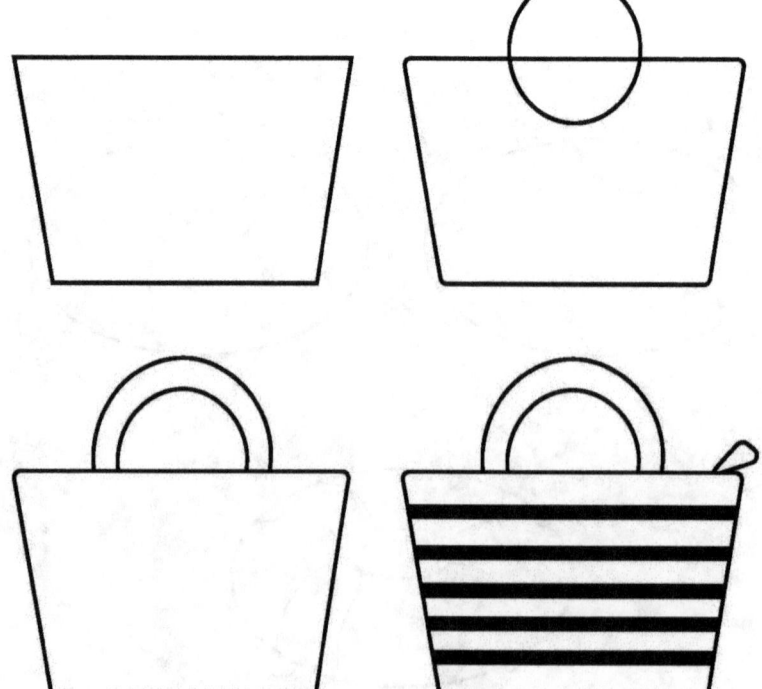

5. SNORKELING GOGGLES

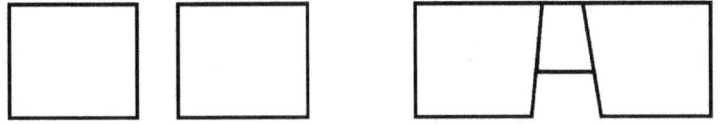
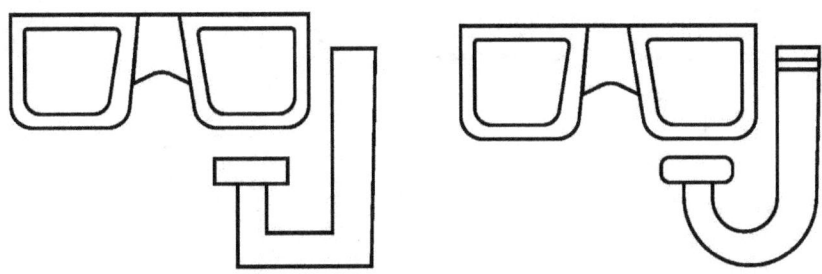

6. SUNSCREEN

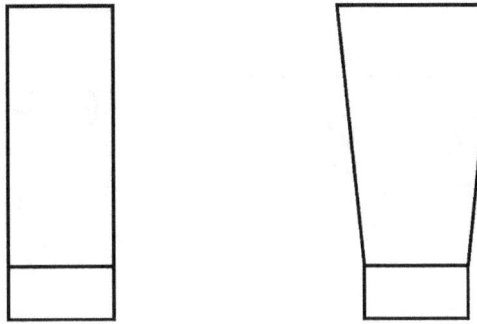
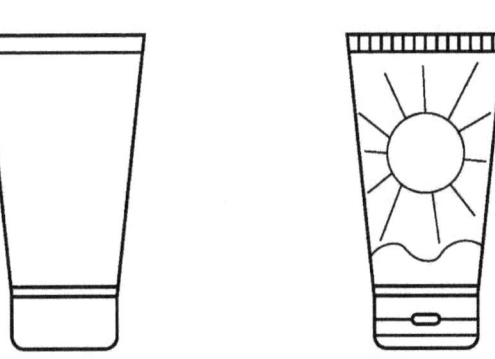

7. SWIMSUIT

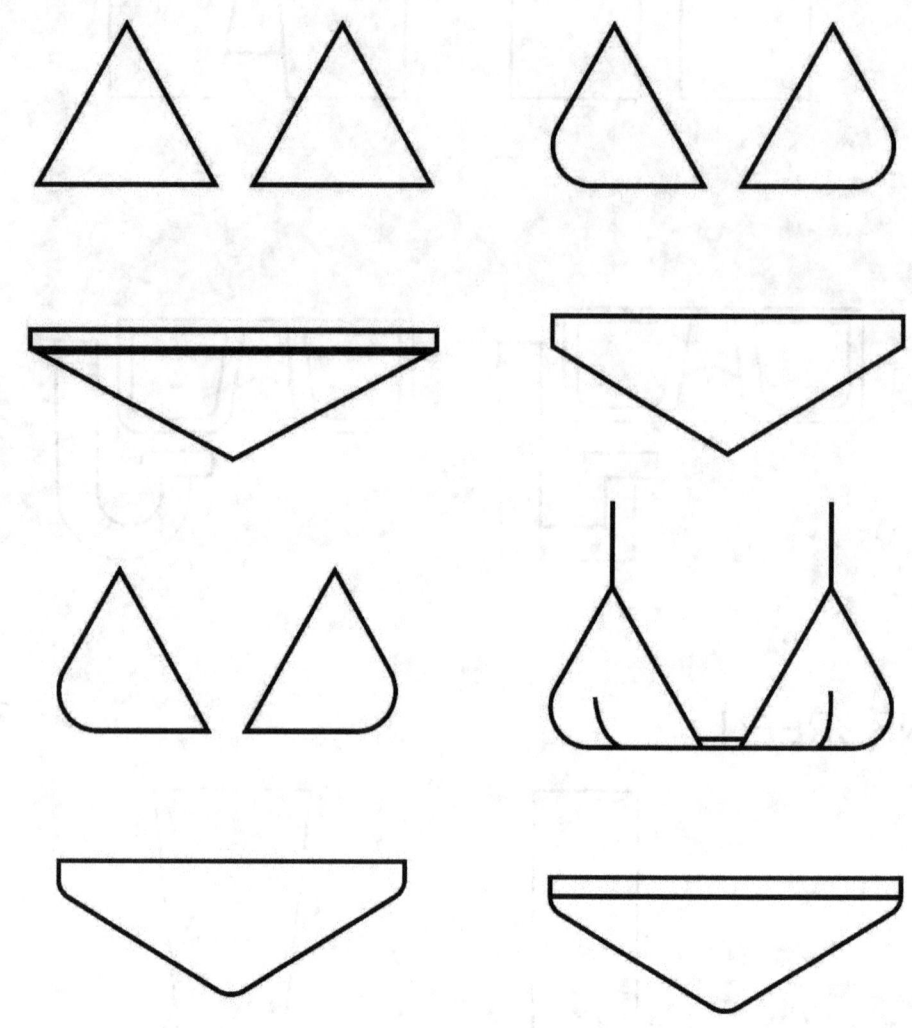

8. FLIP FLOPS

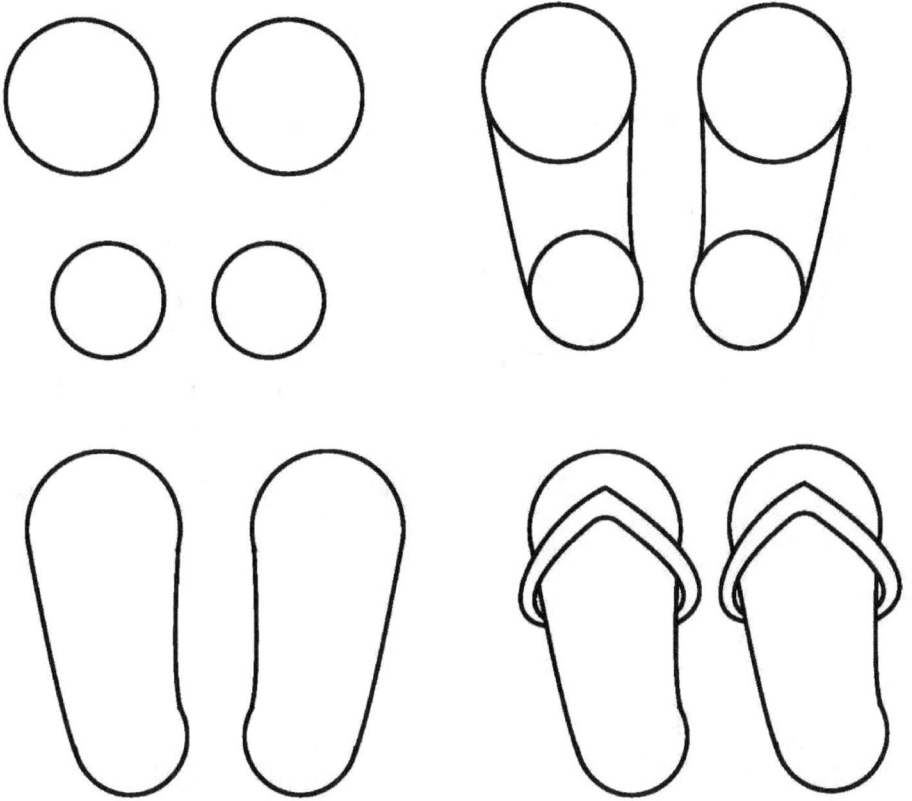

9. SUN HAT

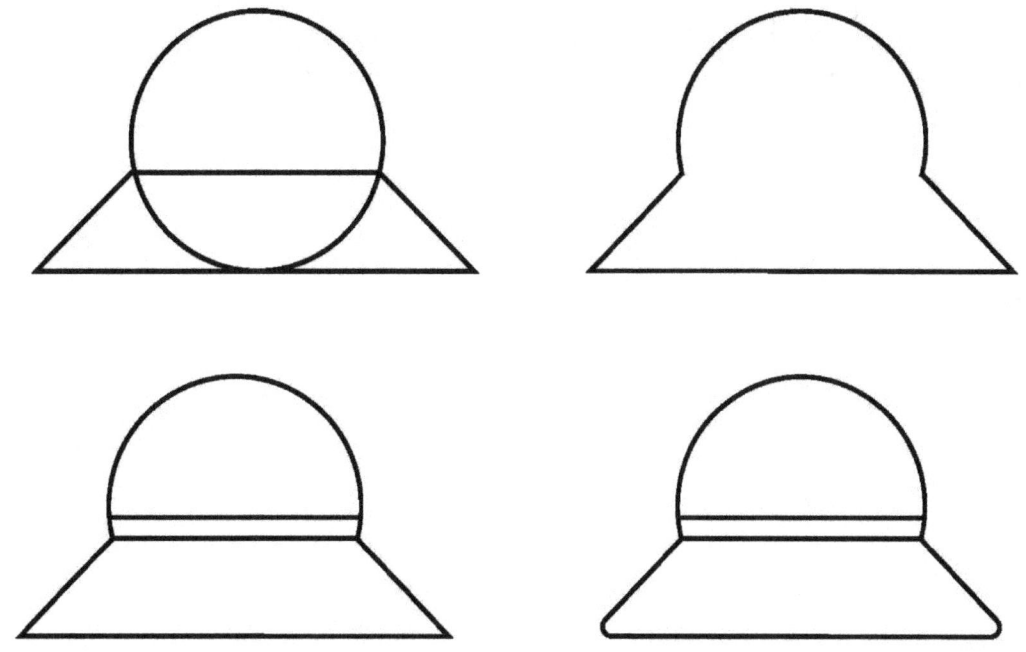

## 10. FLIPPERS

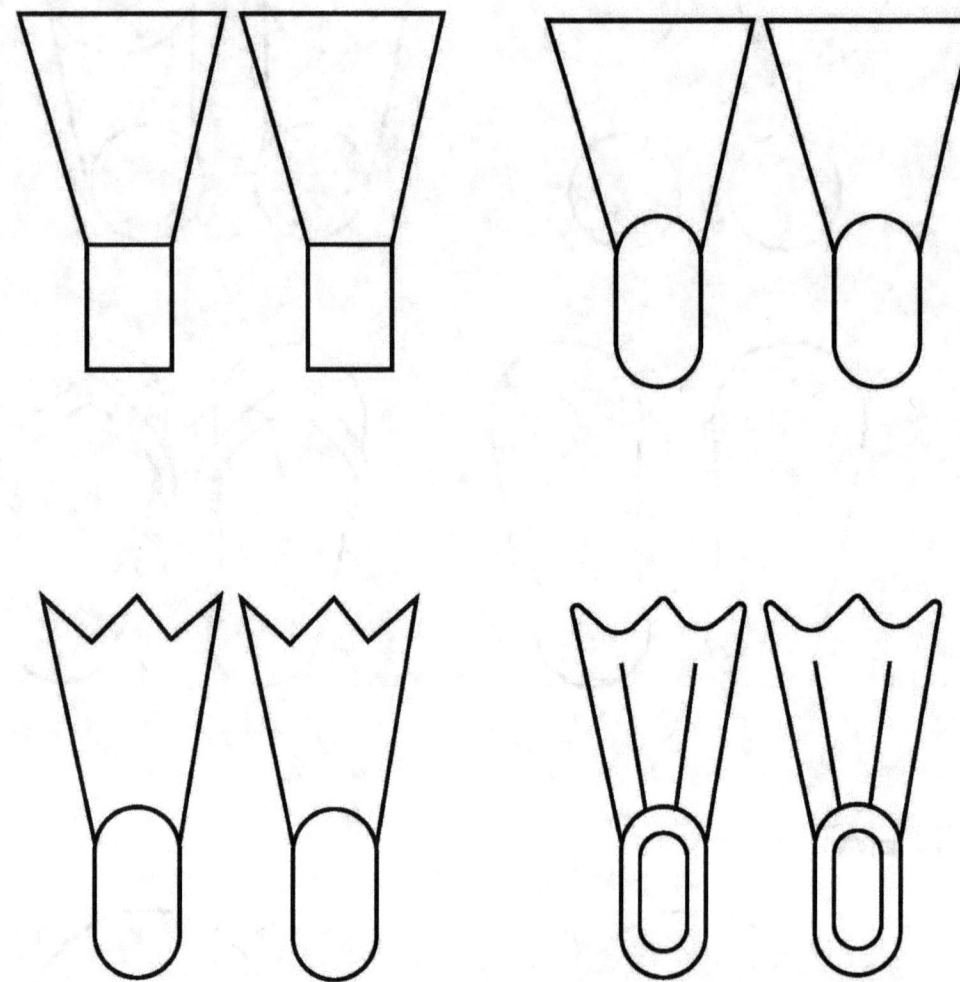

# KAWAII OBJECTS
## FITNESS AND SPORTS

1. **DUMBBELLS**

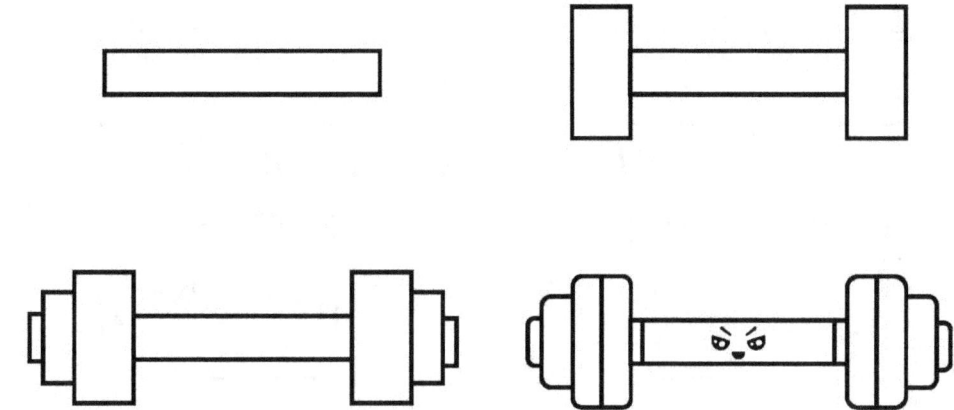

2. **KETTLEBELL**

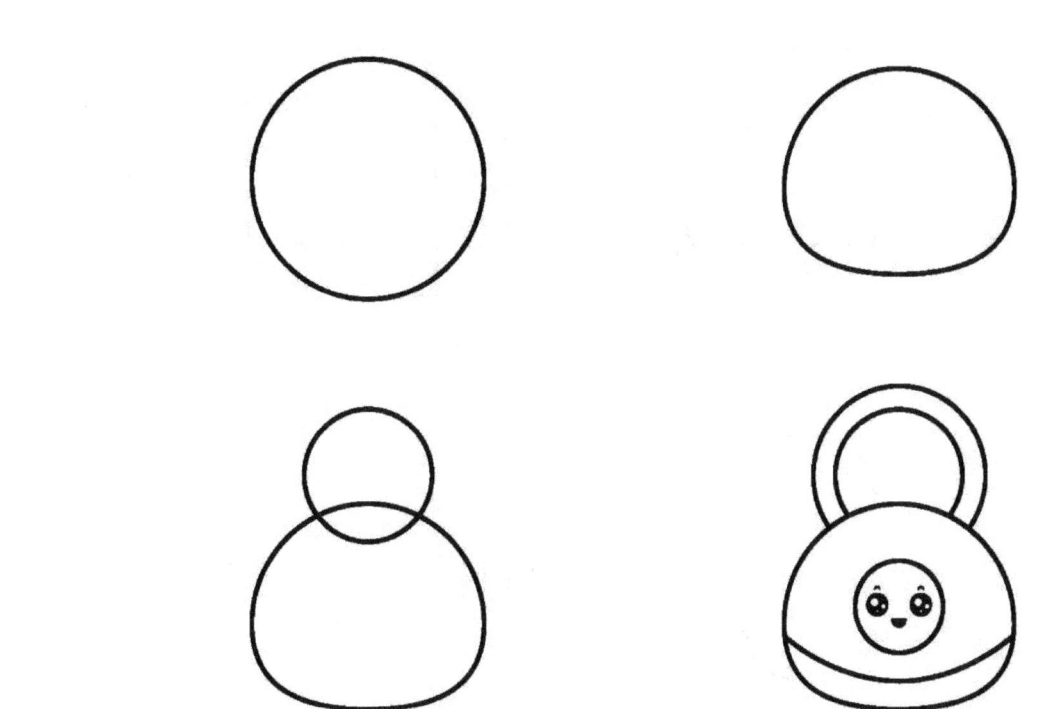

3. WEIGHING SCALE

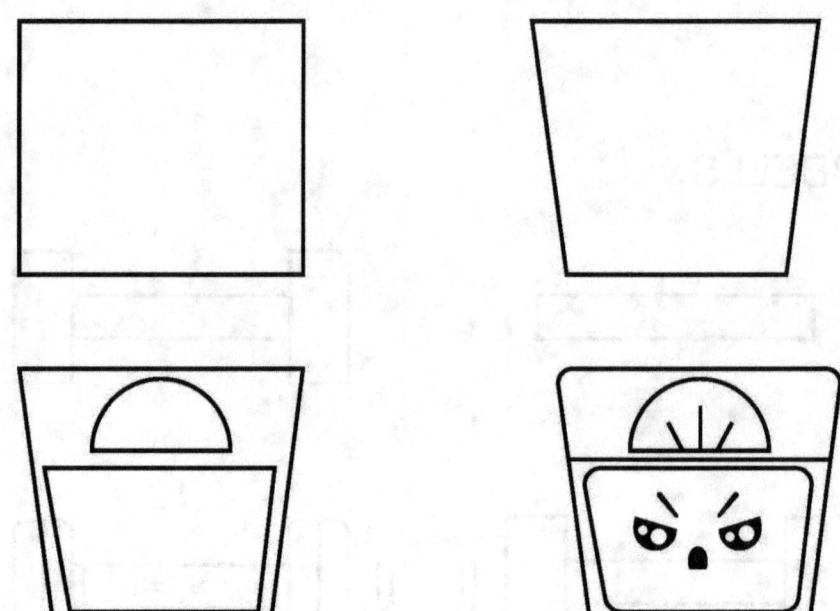

4. BOXING GLOVES

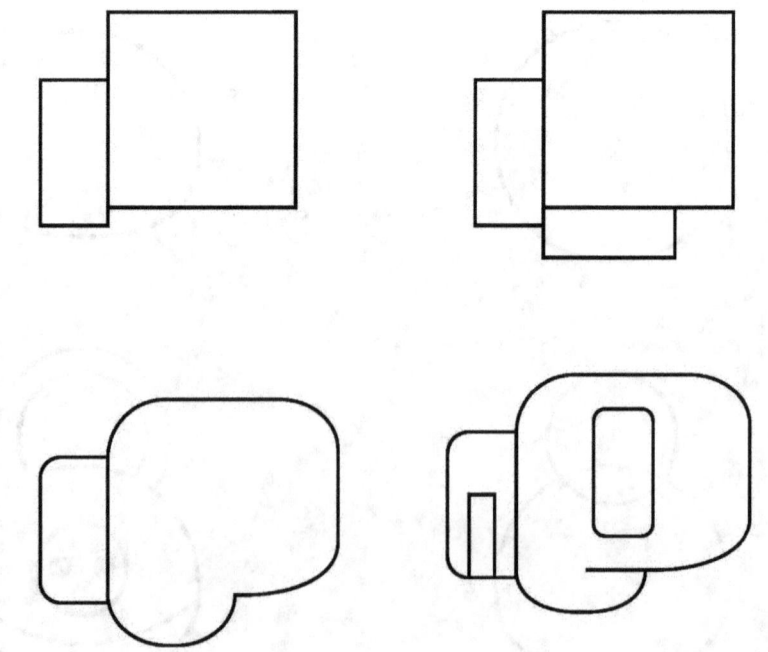

5. FITNESS WATCH

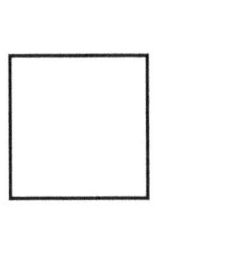
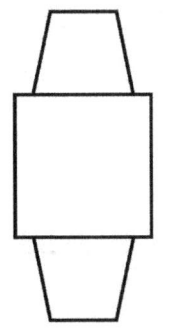
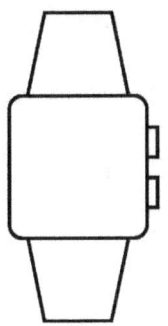
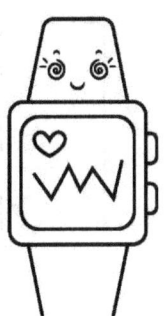

6. FOOTBALL HELMET

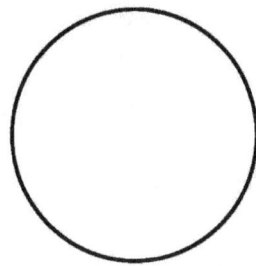
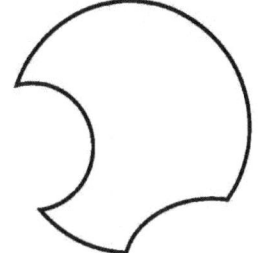
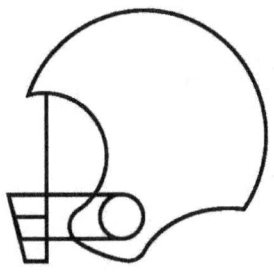
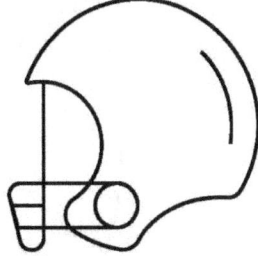

## 7. ENERGY DRINK

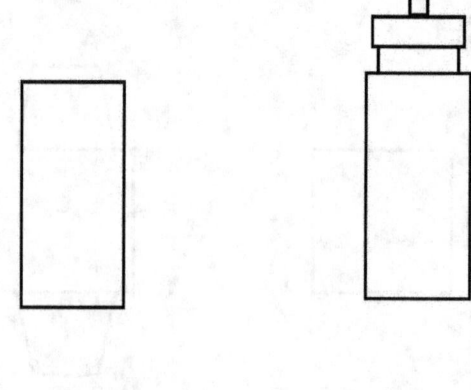
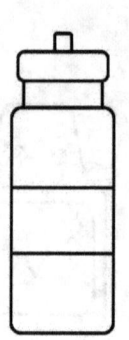

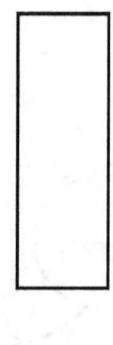
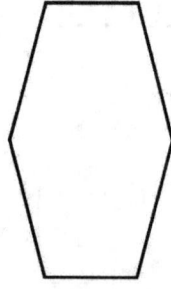

## 8. BOWLING PIN

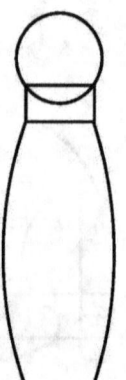
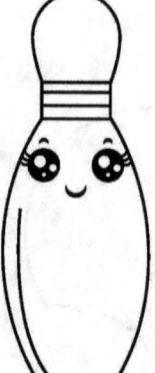

## 9. BASEBALL BAT

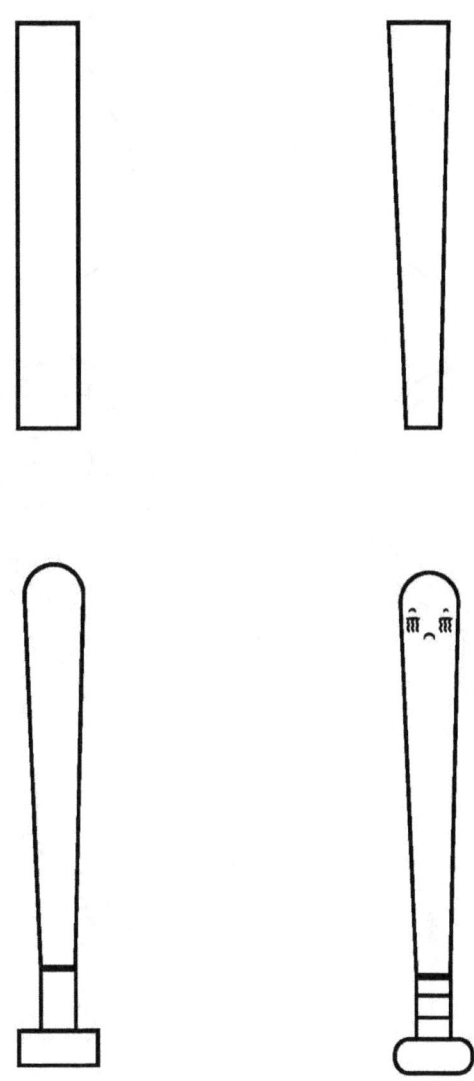

## 10. RACKET

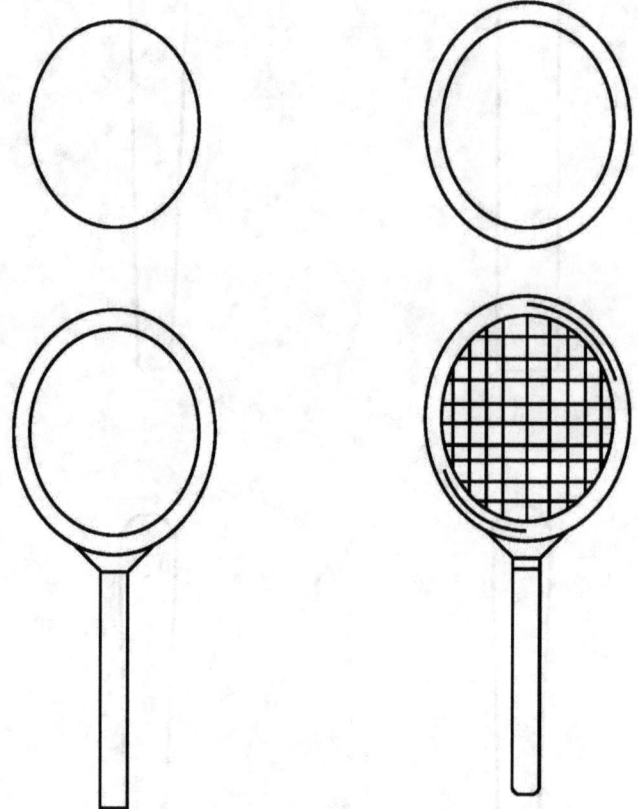

# KAWAII OBJECTS
## TRAVEL THINGS

1. SUITCASE

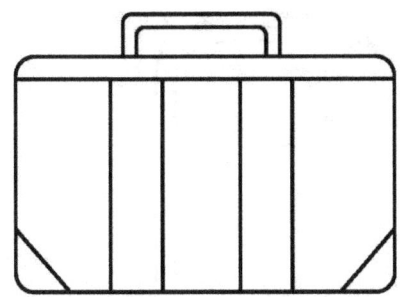
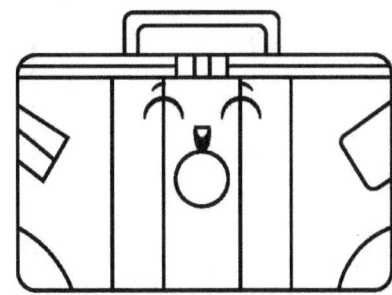

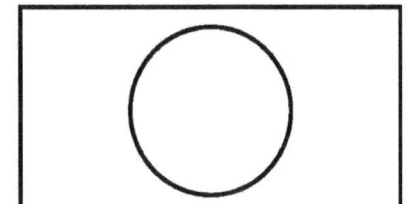

2. CAMERA

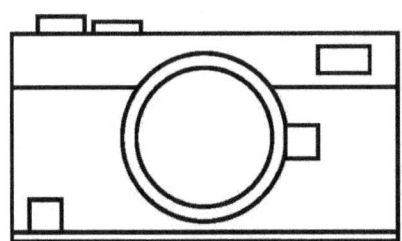
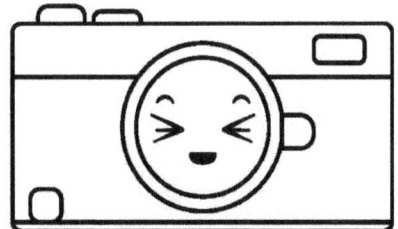

3. LUGGAGE

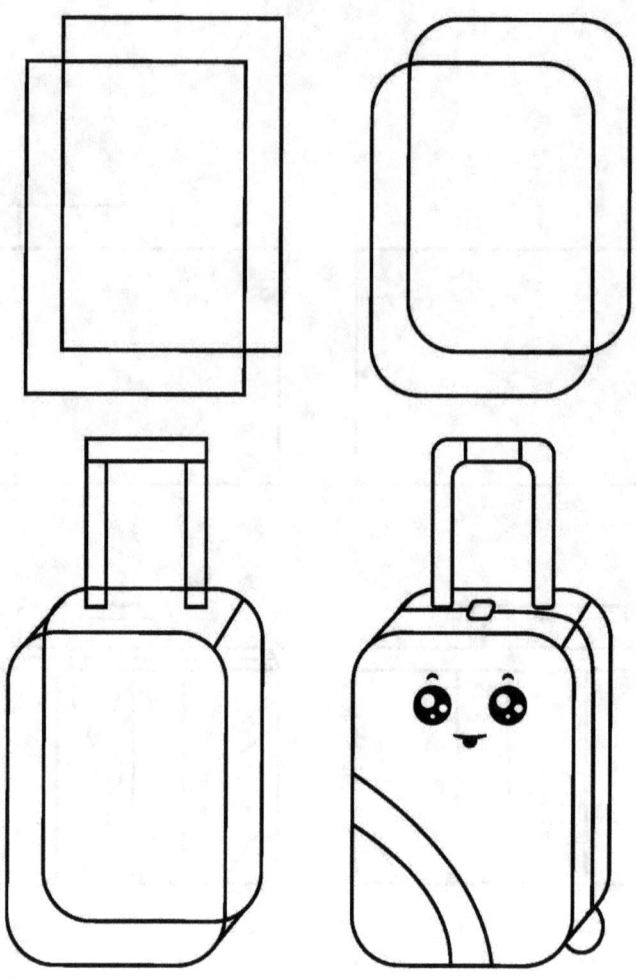

4. TRAVEL JOURNAL

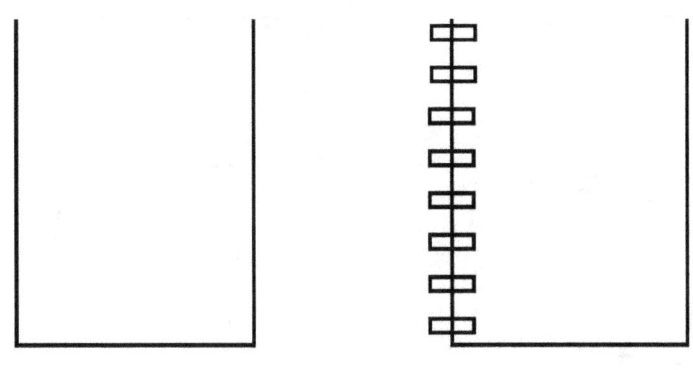

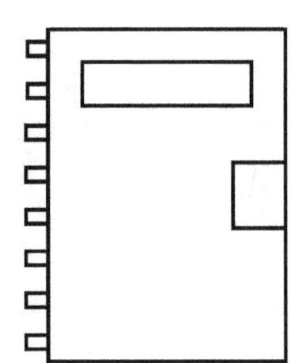 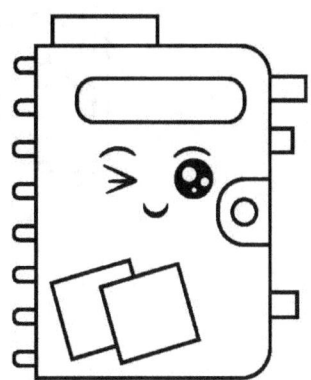

5. SLEEPING MASK

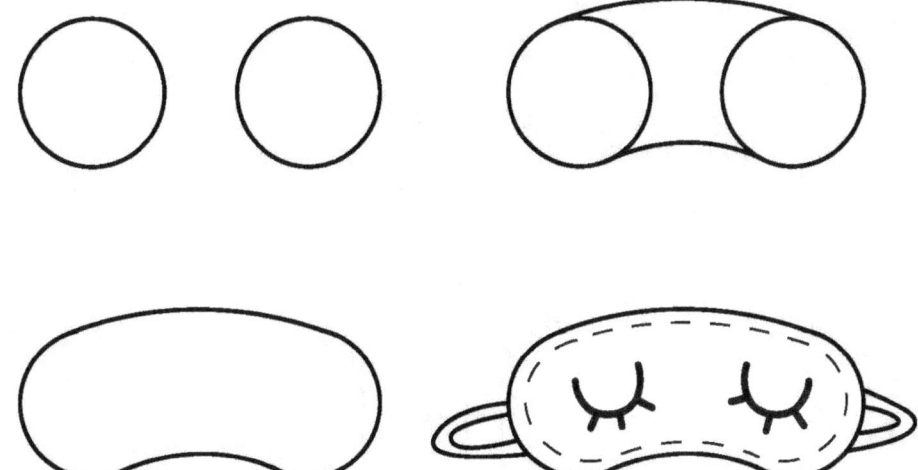

## 6. POSTCARD

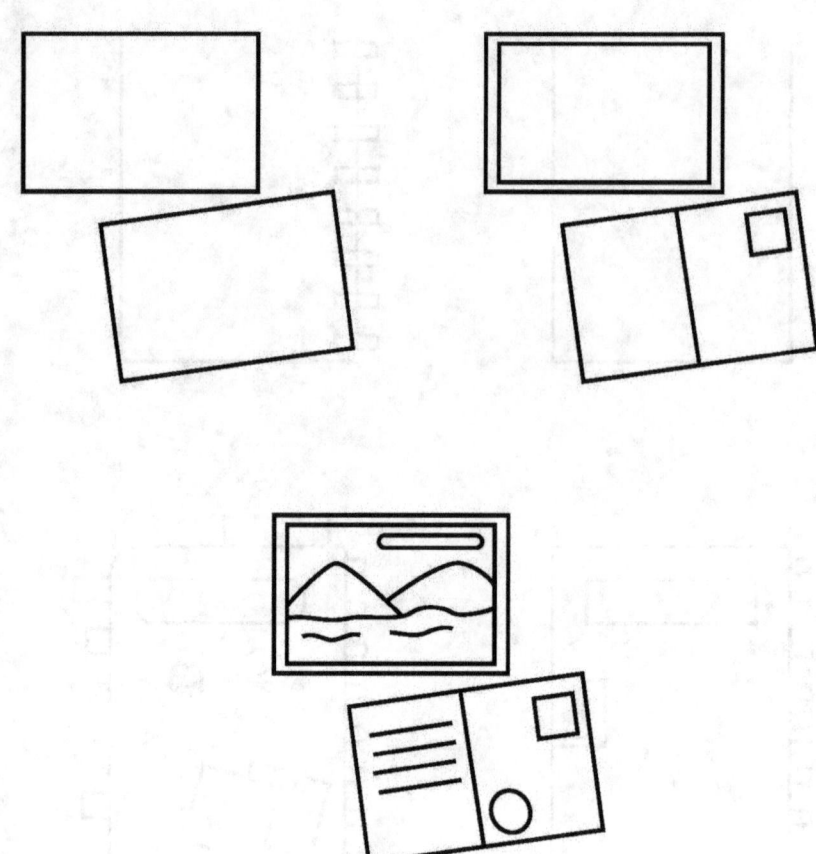

## 7. PASSPORT

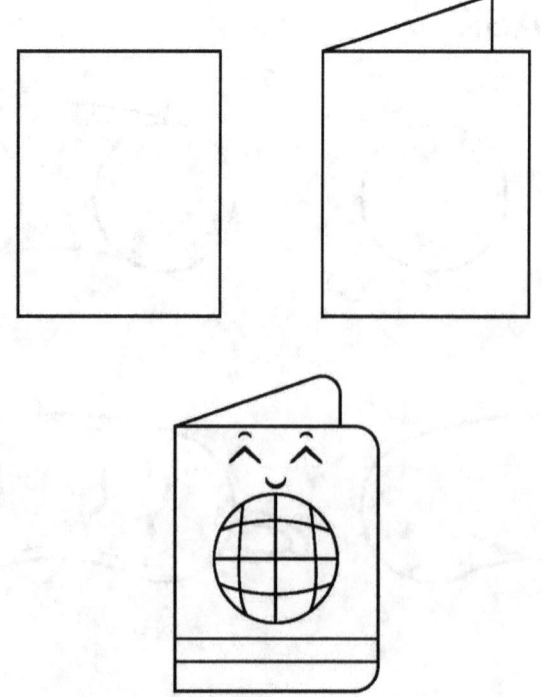

8. MAP

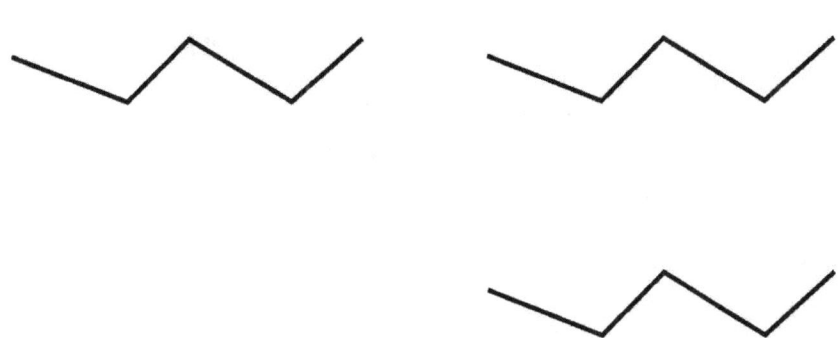

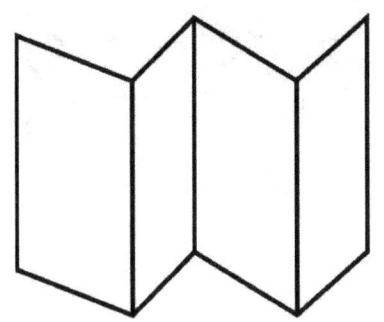 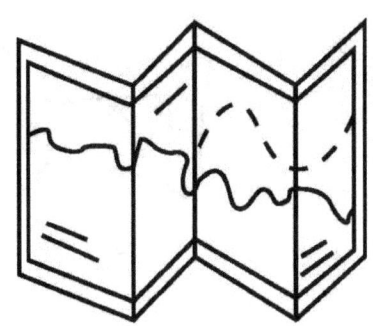

9. COMPASS

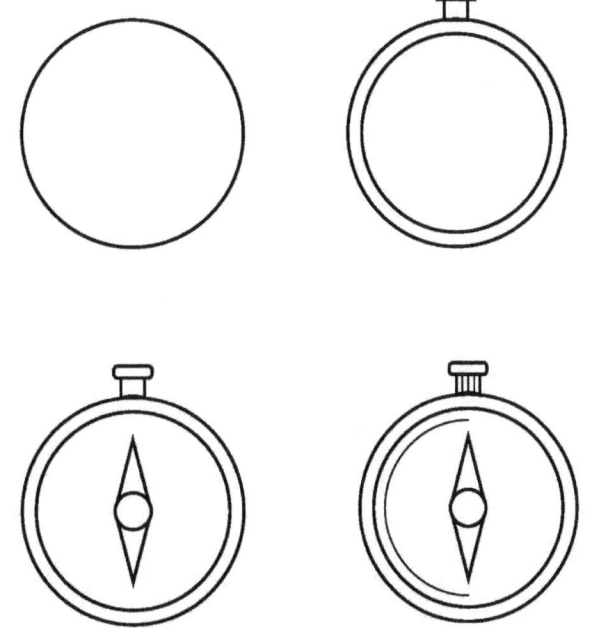

## 10. AIRPLANE

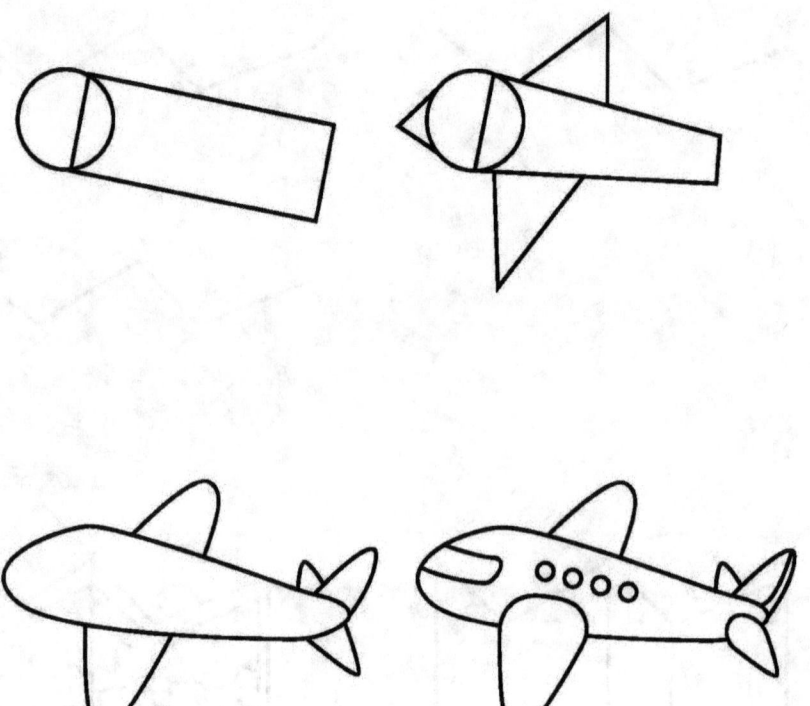

# FINAL WORDS

Now that we have gone over the tutorials in drawing kawaii, it is time to draw them on your own!

Remember the most basic points in drawing kawaii: the lines are thick and round, the details are very simplified, and lastly, adding cute faces and designs like hearts, stars, and lines will instantly make it a lot cuter!

You can add these kawaii drawings to your notes to liven up your lessons or use them to make a cute birthday card for your friend!

Make it even livelier by adding cute colours like pastel colours to amplify the cuteness!

Practice makes perfect! Now go on and draw the cutest animals and chibis!

Keep being kawaii!

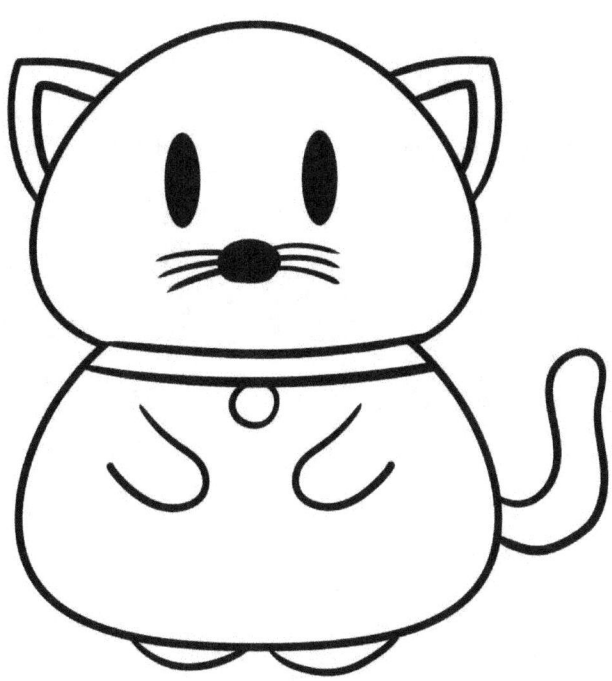

★★★★★

Thank you for getting our book!

If you enjoy using it and you found it useful in your journey
of learning to draw, we would greatly appreciate
your review on Amazon.

Just head on over to this book's Amazon page and click
"Write a customer review".

We read each and every one of them. Thanks!

★★★★★

www.ingramcontent.com/pod-product-compliance
Lightning Source LLC
Chambersburg PA
CBHW060417220526
45465CB00008B/2919